When Men Stand Up

BY

~Lemuel King~

Dedication

To every man who chose to rise when it was easier to stay seated.

To the fathers who showed up.

To the sons who searched for purpose.

To the husbands who learned how to love sacrificially.

To the brothers who stood in the gap.

To the leaders who stayed the course when the weight of responsibility tried to break them.

This book is for the man who failed but got back up.

For the man who cried in silence but still protected his household.

For the man who was never affirmed but still decided to affirm others.

For the man who leads, not with a loud voice, but with a faithful walk.

To the mentors, uncles, coaches, pastors, and everyday men who model quiet strength, unwavering conviction, and relentless love—thank you for showing us what it means to stand up.

And to the next generation of men...

May you never be ashamed to lead with love, walk in truth, honor your commitments, and follow God's voice above the noise of the world.

This book is your blueprint, your mirror, and your charge.

— Lemuel King

Optional Signing Page

I, ______________________________________

(Please print your name)

Having read and reflected on this call to courage,

I commit to stand up for what is right, to lead with integrity,

and to support those around me in their journey.

Signature: ______________________________________

Date: ______________________________________

"May this commitment remind you daily of the strength you carry and the impact you make when you stand up."

— Lemuel King

Table Of Contents

Chapter 1

The Power of Presence

"Watch ye, stand fast in the faith, quit you like men, be strong."
—1 Corinthians 16:13 (KJV)

There is something unshakably powerful about a man who shows up—not with bravado or bluster, but with unwavering presence. He doesn't need a pulpit or a platform. He doesn't need a spotlight or a title. What he carries can't be bought or borrowed—it's born out of conviction, humility, and love.

A man who is present in his home, consistent in his community, and grounded in his faith brings a kind of calm that anchors everything around him. And yet, this kind of presence is in short supply.

In today's culture, where manhood is either attacked, ignored, or misrepresented, it's more critical than ever for men to return to the foundational strength of presence.

Not perfection.

Not production.

Not performance.

But presence.

The Presence Gap

Across our cities, schools, households, and sanctuaries, there is a presence gap—a void left behind not just by missing fathers, but also by emotionally unavailable husbands, disengaged leaders, and discouraged brothers. The gap is not always created through abandonment. Sometimes it forms through wounds. Through shame. Through men never being taught how to stay.

This absence shows up in the eyes of a boy who's trying to figure out who he is by watching entertainers instead of elders. It shows up in the voice of a woman crying out for help while carrying the weight of two roles. It echoes in the silence of churches struggling to keep men engaged. The presence gap isn't just painful—it's generational.

A study by the U.S. Census Bureau revealed that 1 in 4 children live without a father in the home. But those numbers don't tell the whole story. There are men physically in the house who are emotionally checked out.

There are men who show up for work every day, yet haven't shown up for their children's spiritual growth. There are men who lead meetings but won't lead in prayer.

The presence gap is a spiritual crisis.

Men are called to be watchers on the wall, intercessors in their homes, examples to the next generation. But if we're not present—if we're not visible, audible, and engaged— who will our sons model, and who will our daughters trust?

Presence Over Performance

Performance is exhausting. It's a treadmill that never leads to fulfillment.

Men are often praised for their hustle, admired for their grind, and applauded for their achievements. But when all is said and done, nobody asks how many hours you worked. They ask if you were there.

Were you at the game?

Did you listen when your wife broke down?

Did you tuck your children in with prayer and presence?

Did you sit with your brother in his lowest moment?

Did your loved ones feel seen?

Presence doesn't mean having all the answers. It means showing up even when you don't. It's not just doing something for people—it's being with them.

Think about Jesus. He didn't just perform miracles and disappear. He walked with His disciples. He wept at Lazarus' tomb. He ate with tax collectors. He paused for the woman with the issue of blood. He noticed Zacchaeus in a tree. His ministry was fueled not just by power—but by presence.

Showing Up Even When It's Hard

For many men, the hardest place to be is present—especially when shame is knocking.

There are fathers who abandoned their families and now live with silent regret. There are men who buried emotions so deeply that now they don't know how to connect. There are husbands who failed in faithfulness and don't feel worthy to return. There are brothers who disappointed their loved ones and now stand on the sidelines, afraid to try again.

But hear this: There is power in the return.

The enemy will try to convince you that it's too late. That you're too far gone. That nobody wants you back. That showing up now won't make a difference.

He is a liar.

Yes, your presence may not erase your absence—but it can redeem the future.

There's a parable Jesus told about a father who saw his son coming from a distance. The boy had made a mess of his life. He had dishonored his home. But when the father saw him, he didn't turn away. He didn't shame him. He didn't wait for an apology. He ran. Why? Because restoration is more important than reputation.

Brothers, your presence—even if late—is still powerful.

It's time to return. Even if they don't understand at first. Even if the door is barely cracked open. Even if you're met with skepticism. Let your presence speak before your words do.

The Spiritual Presence of a Man

There is no substitute for a man who walks with God.

When a man takes up his spiritual mantle and leads with humility and faith, hell trembles. Not because he's loud.

Not because he's perfect. But because he's aligned with heaven.

A man who intercedes invites divine protection.

A man who worships releases freedom in his household.

A man who studies God's Word provides a moral compass for his children.

A man who repents teaches others the beauty of grace.

Spiritual presence means being sensitive to the Spirit of God and alert to the schemes of the enemy. It's an anointing that says, *"Not in my house. Not on my watch."*

The Bible says in **Job 1:5** that Job regularly offered burnt offerings for each of his children, saying, *"It may be that my sons have sinned, and cursed God in their hearts."* Job was present in the spirit—even when his children weren't.

That is the kind of spiritual presence God is calling us back to.

Presence Is Leadership

Many men think leadership begins with commanding others. In truth, it begins with controlling yourself.

A man who shows up for his family even after a long day is a leader.

A man who keeps his word is a leader.

A man who forgives even when he could retaliate is a leader.

A man who kneels in prayer before he acts is a leader.

Leadership isn't about perfection—it's about being dependable in the dark.

And leadership is never accidental. It's intentional. It requires courage to stay when the enemy says run. It takes humility to admit when you're wrong and strong faith to trust that your presence matters more than your perfection.

Every man reading this has influence. The question is: Are you present enough to use it for good?

A Generational Shift Begins With One Man

You don't have to come from a long line of men who got it right to be the one who gets it right now.

You can be the first in your bloodline to be present.

The first to break the silence.

The first to pray out loud.

The first to hug instead of curse.

The first to raise children in the fear of the Lord.

The first to be healed from past abuse and not pass it forward.

You are not just standing for today—you are standing for tomorrow. You are standing for your sons and your sons' sons. You are standing so that when your name is remembered, it is connected to strength, integrity, and presence.

Scripture Reflection

"Watch ye, stand fast in the faith, quit you like men, be strong."
—1 Corinthians 16:13 (KJV)

This verse is a divine charge: Be alert. Stay grounded. Conduct yourself with strength and maturity. Show up as a man—consistently, prayerfully, lovingly.

Activation Prompt

Think deeply about one area in your life where your presence is absent or inconsistent. It might be with your spouse, your children, your community, or even your spiritual walk.

Write it down. Confess it in prayer. Then take one tangible action this week to close the gap.

Whether it's a phone call, a visit, an apology, or simply sitting in silence with someone who needs you—show up.

Chapter 2

Fatherhood Without Fear

"Like as a father pitieth his children, so the Lord pitieth them that fear him."—**Psalm 103:13 (KJV)**

To be called **"Dad"** is one of the most powerful identities a man can carry. It speaks of responsibility. Legacy. Strength. Tenderness. But for many men, the idea of fatherhood doesn't start with pride—it starts with pressure.

Some fear it.

Some avoid it.

Some fail in it.

Some never got a chance to see what it looked like.

And in that vacuum of experience, culture has stepped in with distorted definitions—teaching men that fatherhood is primarily about how much money you make, how firm your punishments are, or how silent your emotions stay.

But real fatherhood was never meant to be built on fear.

It was designed by God to reflect His nature. His consistency. His compassion. His commitment. Fatherhood is not about ruling a house—it's about covering one. It's not about having control—it's about offering comfort. It's not about power—it's about presence.

Let's confront what many men quietly carry but rarely say out loud: the fear of failing as a father.

The Silent Weight Men Carry

Most fathers won't say it out loud, but they're afraid:

Afraid of not knowing what to say.

Afraid of not being enough.

Afraid of repeating the same mistakes their fathers made.

Afraid of being vulnerable in front of their children.

Afraid of failing in ways they can't fix.

Fear makes men second-guess the very thing God has equipped them to do. It makes them overcompensate— buying things instead of building relationships. It makes them overprotect—controlling instead of connecting. It makes them emotionally rigid—more concerned with obedience than understanding.

But here's the truth: fatherhood is not about being fearless—it's about being faithful, even in fear.

If you feel overwhelmed by the idea of being a father, you're not alone. But you're also not incapable. The moment you accepted the assignment—whether through birth, adoption, marriage, or mentorship—God began equipping you to carry it out.

The Father Wound: Parenting While Bleeding

Many men are fathering while bleeding from wounds they've never acknowledged.

A harsh father who never said *"I love you."*

A physically present but emotionally absent dad.

A stepfather who made you feel like an outsider.

A mentor who abandoned you without warning.

A dad who left and never came back.

These wounds don't disappear just because you became a father yourself. In fact, they often resurface at the worst times—when your child needs comfort, when your teen challenges your authority, when you feel disrespected.

Unhealed wounds lead to unintentional harm.

Sometimes, we lash out—not because of what our children did, but because of what we never dealt with. We distance ourselves—not because they did anything wrong, but because we're scared to be exposed.

But hear me clearly: you are not your father.
And even if your father was a good man, you were not called to repeat—you were called to evolve.

God does not call you to copy dysfunction. He calls you to confront it, heal from it, and build something new.

Breaking the Cycle

Breaking generational cycles is not about blaming the past—it's about choosing a better future.

If your father was absent, you can choose to be present.
If your father was cold, you can choose to be warm.
If your father disciplined without grace, you can choose to lead with both love and correction.

Breaking the cycle means:

Praying even when no one else in your family did.

Holding your children even if you were never held.

Saying *"I'm proud of you"* even if you never heard it yourself.

Sitting with your kids in silence just so they know you're near.

Cycles are broken through consistent decisions—not loud declarations. It's not about being a perfect father in one moment. It's about being a present one over time.

Fatherhood Is Discipleship

A father is more than a protector or provider—he is a teacher of values.

Whether you realize it or not, your children are learning manhood, womanhood, worship, work ethic, respect, and emotional regulation by watching you.

They are watching:

How you talk to their mother

How you respond to stress

How you apologize

How you speak about faith

How you treat people in public

You are either building identity or confusion.

Jesus modeled spiritual fathering with His disciples. He walked with them, taught them, rebuked them with love, restored them, and released them. He didn't demand perfection—He demanded presence and progression.

You can do the same with your children. You're not raising robots. You're discipling future leaders. Don't just discipline them when they're wrong—develop them when they're right.

When You're a Father to Someone Else's Child

Fatherhood is not only biological. There are children, teens, and young adults waiting to be spiritually fathered. Waiting to be seen, affirmed, and challenged in love.

You may be a stepfather, a coach, a teacher, or a big brother-type. Don't underestimate the role you've been given.

You might not have given them your DNA—but you can give them something deeper: your time, your wisdom, your prayers, and your protection.

One conversation. One ride home. One invitation to church. One *"I believe in you"* can shift the trajectory of a child's life.

Fatherhood and Forgiveness

If you've failed as a father—missed birthdays, raised your voice in anger, made mistakes—you are not beyond redemption.

What your child may need most is not your defense—it's your humility.

"I'm sorry."

"I was wrong."

"I should've been there."

"I'm working to do better."

These aren't just words—they're seeds of healing.

And if your child isn't ready to receive you yet, don't stop being available. Let your repentance be louder than your regret. Pray for the door to open—but be ready to walk through it in love when it does.

Forgiveness is possible. But it often begins with you.

The Father's Voice

In a world filled with loud opinions and digital noise, your voice—your fatherly voice—still matters.

Don't let culture raise your children. Don't let the internet define their worth. Don't let their friends teach them about identity.

Your words are spiritual armor.

Speak blessings over your children every day. Call out their gifts. Correct them with gentleness. Challenge them with love. Cover them in prayer.

When they remember you decades from now, let it not be for the discipline alone—but for the declarations you made over their lives.

Fathering Through Seasons

Your role as a father will evolve.

In childhood: they need your attention.

In adolescence: they need your boundaries and belief.

In adulthood: they need your wisdom, support, and release.

Don't try to father every season the same way. Ask God for discernment in how to show up. Remain present, even as their needs shift.

Scripture Reflection

"Like as a father pitieth his children, so the Lord pitieth them that fear him."—**Psalm 103:13 (KJV)**

God doesn't parent us with cold distance. He is near. He sees our weaknesses and responds with mercy. Let that be the model for your fatherhood. Not perfection—but compassion.

Activation Prompt

List three things your father never said that you wish he had.

Then say them—to your child, your mentee, or even the younger version of yourself in prayer.

Write them down. Speak them out loud. Then commit to repeating those affirmations regularly.

You are not just raising children. You are raising a legacy.

Chapter 3

Strength Under Control: The Myth of Masculinity

"He hath shewed thee, O man, what is good; and what doth the Lord require of thee, but to do justly, and to love mercy, and to walk humbly with thy God?" – **Micah 6:8 (KJV)**

Some men live trying to prove how strong they are. They wear strength like armor — hard, impenetrable, and heavy.

They confuse volume with authority, dominance with leadership, and silence with maturity.

They were taught to *"man up,"* but not to grow up.

And here's the result: generations of men who are strong on the outside but crushed on the inside. Men who can bench press hundreds of pounds but can't carry their own insecurities. Men who fear vulnerability more than failure. Men who would rather suffer silently than admit they need help.

But God never called men to be hard. He called them to be holy.

He never told us to dominate. He told us to serve.
And He never defined masculinity by ego — but by humility, courage, and control.

Redefining Strength

What is strength?

Strength is not just physical. It's not just loud. And it's not just about being in charge.

Strength is the ability to remain grounded when everything around you is shaking.

It's choosing peace when you want to rage.

It's choosing integrity when temptation calls.

It's stepping forward when fear says hide.

It's forgiving when bitterness says strike back.

Controlled strength is not weakness — it's wisdom.

The strongest men I've ever met have cried in front of their families. They've apologized to their children. They've admitted when they were wrong. And instead of losing respect — they gained it.

Real men don't lose power by being vulnerable. They multiply it.

The Destructive Myth of *"Toxic Toughness"*

The world has sold us a lie: that toughness equals masculinity.

But toughness without tenderness becomes trauma.

Confidence without compassion becomes control.

Leadership without love becomes manipulation.

When men try to bury emotion, it doesn't die — it festers. When we suppress pain, it comes out in our parenting.

When we hide fear, it emerges in anger.

When we avoid accountability, it breeds pride.

Toxic masculinity isn't just a cultural term — it's a spiritual distortion. It's what happens when strength is uncoupled from character.

The goal isn't to be less masculine. The goal is to be biblically masculine — to embody the kind of strength that Jesus walked in: humble, sacrificial, servant-hearted, and unwavering.

Strength as Jesus Modeled It

Jesus is the greatest example of controlled strength the world has ever seen.

He had the power to call down angels — but He chose to carry a cross.

He had the right to defend Himself — but He remained silent before His accusers.

He had nothing to prove — and still proved everything through love.

Jesus wasn't fragile. He wasn't passive. He wasn't timid.

He was strong enough to submit to the will of the Father.

Strong enough to forgive those who beat Him.

Strong enough to weep in public.

Strong enough to kneel before His disciples and wash their feet.

That's manhood. That's leadership. That's divine strength in action.

Field Notes: When Strength Hurts

I met a father who raised his boys to never cry. *"Real men keep it together,"* he said.

But as his sons got older, they didn't turn into leaders.

They turned into strangers.

They didn't run to him with pain — they hid from him.

They didn't share their struggles — they numbed them.

And by the time he wanted to reconnect, they had built emotional walls too tall to scale.

He had modeled strength — but not safety. And eventually, they began to equate masculinity with suppression instead of self-control.

After years of prayer and rebuilding, that same father stood in front of his sons one day, eyes full of tears, and said, *"I'm sorry. I was wrong. I want to be a different kind of strong."*

And in that moment, they didn't see weakness. They saw a man finally willing to stand.

Self-Control Is the Standard

Biblical manhood is never about being uncontrollable. In fact, self-control is one of the fruits of the Spirit *(Galatians 5:22–23).*

A man without self-control is like a car with no brakes — powerful, fast, and dangerous.

When a man learns to control:

his mouth — he becomes trustworthy.

his anger — he becomes safe.

his urges — he becomes honorable.

his emotions — he becomes stable.

his decisions — he becomes wise.

God doesn't call men to be soft. He calls them to be submitted. And submission produces fruit that raw strength never could.

Scripture Foundations

"He that is slow to anger is better than the mighty; and he that ruleth his spirit than he that taketh a city." – **Proverbs 16:32 (KJV)**

"Be strong and of a good courage, fear not, nor be afraid of them: for the LORD thy God, he it is that doth go with thee..." – **Deuteronomy 31:6 (KJV)**

"The meek shall inherit the earth..." – **Matthew 5:5 (KJV)**

Daily Markers of Strength Under Control

Want to see if you're walking in controlled strength? Ask yourself daily:

Did I pause before I reacted?

Did I speak life, not just truth?

Did I protect someone's heart, even if I was right?

Did I lead with prayer — or with pressure?

Did I choose discipline over impulse?

Pause and Reflect

When was the last time your strength hurt someone you love?

Where in your life are you relying on pressure instead of peace?

Who needs to hear an apology, not an explanation?

What would change if you saw strength as restraint instead of reaction?

Prayer of Realignment

Father, thank You for creating me in Your image — strong, capable, and called. But I confess that I've sometimes misused my strength. I've tried to control when I should have submitted. I've responded in pride when I should have paused in prayer. Teach me how to lead with love, how to protect with peace, and how to reflect Jesus in all I do. Let my strength be governed by Your Spirit and guided by Your Word. In Jesus' name, amen.

Final Words: Strength that Serves

The strongest man in the room isn't always the loudest. He's the one who serves without needing credit, leads without seeking control, and stands without stepping on others.

Strength under control is not just a skill — it's a legacy. And when men walk in it, families heal. Churches flourish. Communities shift.

And the next generation sees a new picture of what it means to be a man.

Chapter 4

Fathers, Sons, and the Fight for Identity

"And lo a voice from heaven, saying, This is my beloved Son, in whom I am well pleased." **– Matthew 3:17 (KJV)**

Some men spend their entire lives chasing two things: A name… and a nod.

A name that confirms their identity.

A nod of approval that says, *"You matter. You have what it takes."*

And for many, that pursuit doesn't start in adulthood — it begins as a boy, looking up at a father who either affirms him or leaves him asking forever.

The fight for identity is not a modern issue. It's a generational one. It's not just a psychological matter — it's spiritual warfare. Because if the enemy can confuse a man about who he is, he can manipulate how he lives.

This is why fatherhood is sacred. Why legacy matters. And why silence is never neutral.

The Wounds That Shape a Man

Many of the struggles men face aren't rooted in weakness — they're rooted in wounds.

Unspoken, unprocessed, and unresolved.

A man may look confident, but beneath the surface:

He's trying to prove he's worth something.

He's trying to outpace a voice that said he'd never be enough.

He's trying to earn affection that should have been freely given.

He's fighting battles handed to him by a father who never fought his own.

These wounds don't heal with age. They morph. They hide. And eventually, they leak out — in how a man raises his kids, relates to his spouse, handles failure, or avoids intimacy.

The identity battle begins at home.

And it often starts with a father who couldn't say:

"You're my son. I love you. I'm proud of you."

Fathers Reflect Identity

Every father, whether he realizes it or not, is a reflection of God — or a distortion of Him.

That's why a father's blessing carries supernatural weight.

When a father:

speaks identity, his children walk boldly.

shows affection, they feel secure.

disciplines with love, they grow with wisdom.

listens without judgment, they learn to trust.

But when a father is absent — physically, emotionally, or spiritually — the child begins to search. For guidance. For grounding. For value.

If he can't find it in the home, he'll find it in:

the streets

the screen

the gangs

the internet

the applause

the arms of someone who doesn't care about his soul

Fathers, whether broken or strong, shape destinies.

The Danger of the Silent Father

Some men were wounded not by what was said — but by what was never said.

No *"I love you."*

No *"I'm proud of you."*

No *"I see greatness in you."*

Just silence. Distance. Tasks. Expectations.

And in the absence of affirmation, boys become men with questions still echoing in their hearts.

The silent father teaches without words:

"You're only valuable when you perform."

"Emotion makes you weak."

"If I don't say I'm proud, you must not be worthy."

The son learns to:

suppress instead of speak.

survive instead of thrive.

achieve instead of receive.

But deep down, he's not chasing money — he's chasing a moment with his father that never happened.

God's Model of Fatherhood

Let's return to Jesus.

Before He preached a sermon…

Before He walked on water…

Before He carried the cross…

His Father said:

"This is my beloved Son, in whom I am well pleased." – **Matthew 3:17**

This declaration came before any public accomplishment.

God the Father didn't say, *"I'm proud because of what You've done."*

He said, *"I'm proud because of who You are."*

That's true fatherhood — identity before performance.

Affirmation before expectation.

Love without condition.

This wasn't just a moment of affection. It was a model.

One that every man must follow — especially those raising sons or mentoring young men.

Field Notes: A Moment That Changed a Man

I once met a 16-year-old named Brandon who had been suspended three times in one semester. Angry. Withdrawn. Aggressive. The school labeled him a *"behavior problem."*

But when I pulled him aside and asked, *"What's really going on?"*, he broke down.

"My father has a new family. He forgot about me."

That wasn't rebellion. That was a wound.
Not a bad kid — just a hurting son.

Over the next few months, I poured into him. I affirmed him. I corrected him with grace. I saw him — the real him. And slowly, he stood taller. He calmed down. He smiled more. His teachers noticed.

The difference wasn't punishment — it was presence.
One man stepping into the space another man left vacant.

For Every Man Without a Father

Maybe your dad left. Or maybe he was there but never really ***"there."***

Maybe you're reading this as a grown man who still wonders, *"Why wasn't I enough?"*

Let me say this clearly:

You are enough — because God says so.

You are His son. His beloved. His chosen.

And He's proud of you — not for what you've done, but for who you are in Him.

Even if your earthly father never gave you the blessing, your Heavenly Father offers it freely.

"A father of the fatherless... is God in his holy habitation." – **Psalm 68:5**

Breaking Generational Silence

You don't have to repeat what you didn't receive.

If you never heard "I love you," you can still say it.
If you were never affirmed, you can become the one who affirms.

If you were wounded, you can choose to walk in healing — and be a healer.

You are not stuck in your history. You are called to build a new legacy.

For Fathers, Mentors, and Men Who Stand in the Gap

You don't need a biological connection to speak into someone's life.

God may be calling you to father the fatherless.

To see young men who feel invisible.

To speak destiny over the confused, the angry, the broken.

You don't need to be perfect — just present.

A text, a handshake, a prayer, a lunch, a *"You've got greatness in you"* can shift a boy's trajectory.

Affirmation is a weapon. Use it. Speak it. Write it. Repeat it.

Scripture Foundation

"He shall turn the heart of the fathers to the children, and the heart of the children to their fathers…" – **Malachi 4:6**

"The just man walketh in his integrity: his children are blessed after him." – **Proverbs 20:7**

"As a father pitieth his children, so the Lord pitieth them that fear him." – **Psalm 103:13**

Practical Affirmation Phrases for Fathers and Mentors

Say them. Write them. Live them.

"You don't have to earn my love. You already have it."

"I believe in you — even when you're struggling."

"You're not perfect, but you're still mine."

"You have a purpose. Don't let the world define you."

"Even when you fall, I'm still here."

Reflection & Activation

What lies did you believe about yourself growing up — and are they still shaping your identity today?

How has your earthly father's presence or absence affected how you lead, love, and parent?

Who around you needs to hear words you never heard?

What can you do today to bless the next generation — spiritually, emotionally, practically?

Prayer of Healing and Blessing

Heavenly Father, thank You for never leaving me, even when others did. I surrender the wounds from my past — the silence, the rejection, the harsh words, or the absence. Heal what was broken in me. Restore what was lost. I receive my identity as Your beloved son. And now I choose to stand in the gap. Help me bless, lead, and affirm others as You have done for me. Let my voice be one of healing, not harm. Let my life break the cycle. In Jesus' name, amen.

Chapter 5

When Men Love Right: Healing Through Leadership

"Husbands, love your wives, even as Christ also loved the church, and gave himself for it." – **Ephesians 5:25 (KJV)**

The Power in Love That Leads

When a man loves right, he doesn't lose strength—he gains significance.

He doesn't lead by domination or demand, but by dedication and devotion.

His strength is not found in how loudly he speaks, but in how deeply he serves.

His love is not shallow—it's sacrificial.

Real love knows how to cover, how to correct without crushing, and how to stay when others walk away.

The world has told men that leadership is about being feared. But the Word of God teaches that leadership begins with love.

Leadership that heals starts with love that costs.

Love Is a Leadership Assignment

The first role God gave Adam was not just to tend the Garden, but to guard what was entrusted to him.
He was given a role as protector, covering, and presence.

But when love is absent—or out of balance—men abdicate their role. And the people around them begin to pay the price.

When men love right:

They protect without controlling.

They guide without gaslighting.

They serve without seeking credit.

They lead without losing the heart of those they lead.

Love doesn't weaken a man's leadership—it legitimizes it.

The Foundation: Love That Builds, Not Breaks

Homes fall apart when love is missing, misguided, or misapplied.

Love without discipline becomes indulgence.

Love without presence becomes confusion.

Love without truth becomes tolerance of harm.

But love rooted in Christlikeness:

Builds character in children.

Strengthens marriages.

Restores dignity to the broken.

Heals trauma that silence couldn't.

A man who loves right is a man who builds lasting foundations.

Love and the Healing Cycle

Love becomes a healing force when it shows up consistently, even after failure, hurt, or tension.

God doesn't just feel love toward us—He demonstrated it. *(Romans 5:8)*

Jesus didn't just give advice—He gave Himself.

When men love right:

Forgiveness replaces resentment.

Grace becomes more powerful than guilt.

Listening becomes more important than control.

Apologies become normal, not rare.

In many homes, the breakthrough doesn't come through correction—it comes through a father's hug, a husband's humility, or a mentor's affirmation.

Healing begins when love steps in.

Field Notes: A Husband's Turning Point

A man once told me, *"I provide everything. I don't understand why she's pulling away."*

We discovered he was showing up physically, but not emotionally. His leadership was efficient—but not affectionate.

He rarely said "I love you."

He was quick to give instructions, but slow to listen.

He wanted honor, but hadn't created safety.

Over time, he began praying over his wife—out loud. He started affirming her, even when they disagreed. He stopped *"fixing"* her feelings and started feeling with her.

Within months, the atmosphere in their home changed. She smiled again. The kids relaxed. The tension lifted.

Why?

Because love became the language of leadership, not control.

Leadership by Love in Action

1. In Marriage

Loving right means being gentle when irritated, affirming when disappointed, and faithful when tested.

2. In Fatherhood

Loving right means being available—not just physically, but emotionally. It means showing affection and speaking identity.

3. In Friendship

Loving right means holding your brothers accountable and also encouraging them. Iron sharpens iron—not by friction alone, but by careful shaping.

4. In Ministry

Loving right means serving, not spotlighting. It means washing feet before raising voices. Leading from the back before being seen out front.

Jesus: Love that Led the World

Jesus didn't bark orders. He invited. He modeled.

He touched lepers no one would speak to.

He restored women the world wanted to shame.

He wept with Mary and Martha.

He knelt to wash the disciples' feet—including Judas.

"Having loved his own which were in the world, he loved them unto the end." – **John 13:1 (KJV)**

That's love. That's leadership. That's legacy.

And that's the blueprint for every man who dares to love right.

The Cost of Not Loving Right

Men who lead without love often leave:

Wives who are emotionally shut down.

Children who confuse obedience with value.

Teams who perform under pressure but burn out in silence.

Churches that grow in size but shrink in grace.

Leadership without love is just control in disguise.

Love is not optional—it's essential.

It's not a bonus—it's the basis of biblical manhood.

Reflection: What Loving Right Might Require

Humbling yourself and saying, *"I was wrong."*

Slowing down enough to listen—without fixing.

Saying *"I love you"* without waiting for perfection.

Choosing prayer instead of punishment.

Asking God to break the walls pride built over time.

Sometimes loving right is inconvenient. It stretches your ego, your patience, your routine. But it always leads to breakthrough.

Scripture Foundation

"Let all your things be done with charity." – **1 Corinthians 16:14 (KJV)**

"But the fruit of the Spirit is love..." – **Galatians 5:22 (KJV)**

"Love worketh no ill to his neighbour: therefore love is the fulfilling of the law." – **Romans 13:10 (KJV)**

"Love never faileth..." – **1 Corinthians 13:8 (KJV)**

Reflection Questions

What did love look like in the household you grew up in?

In what ways have you confused control with love?

Who in your life needs to experience your love—not in words, but in action?

What would your home, your friendships, or your ministry look like if love truly led everything you did?

Prayer of Love-Driven Leadership

Father, thank You for loving me unconditionally, sacrificially, and faithfully. I confess that I've led from pride, performance, or fear. I want to lead with love—the kind that heals, the kind that listens, the kind that reflects You. Teach me how to love my family, my friends, and my community like You love me. Let my love produce peace, not pressure. Legacy, not fear. Make my leadership soft enough to restore and strong enough to guide. In Jesus' name, amen.

Chapter 6

Taking Responsibility: Owning the Outcome

"For every man shall bear his own burden." – **Galatians 6:5 (KJV)**

The Most Masculine Move a Man Can Make

In a world where image dominates, ego drives, and pride performs, taking responsibility has become a rare—and revolutionary—act of manhood.

Responsibility isn't glamorous. It won't get applause. It often starts in silence.

But a responsible man doesn't need validation—he walks in conviction.

He doesn't lead to be praised—he leads because someone must.

The truth?

What you refuse to own will eventually own you.

Your silence will turn into someone else's suffering.

Your avoidance will become someone else's emotional inheritance.

The moment you stop saying, *"That's not my fault,"* and start saying, "That's still my responsibility,"—that's the moment you become a man worth following.

The Difference Between a Grown Male and a Grown Man

There's a difference between age and maturity.

There are grown males who've never matured past their disappointments.

Men with muscles but no discipline.

Men with jobs but no accountability.

Men with kids but no spiritual covering.

Responsibility is the threshold of maturity. It's not just owning your mess—it's stewarding your mission.

Grown males react.

Grown men respond.

Grown males protect their image.

Grown men protect what matters.

Grown males say, *"It's not my fault."*

Grown men say, *"It's still my job."*

How Responsibility Restores

Responsibility is a spiritual door that leads to:

Reputation repair

Relational restoration

Internal peace

God's favor

Why? Because when a man repents and owns his role, Heaven moves on his behalf.

Think about the Prodigal Son.

It wasn't until he said, *"I have sinned against heaven and against you"* that the Father ran to him.

God does not bless the man who hides behind pride. He blesses the man who humbles himself and takes the walk back.

Why Men Avoid Ownership

Let's get honest.

1. Pride

Men are taught that admitting weakness makes you look soft. So we fake strength and deny struggle—until it poisons our relationships.

2. Shame

Responsibility reminds you of what you should've done. And instead of fixing it, some men run from it. But what you refuse to face, you'll repeat.

3. Fear of Rejection

Some men believe: *"If I admit this, I'll be punished or pushed away."*

So instead, they stay quiet and hope time will fix what truth never addressed.

But truth is not your enemy—it's your rescue.

What Happens When You Don't Own the Outcome

Your wife becomes emotionally exhausted while you stay emotionally unavailable.

Your children become confused by your silence and model your passivity.

Your calling becomes delayed while your comfort stays protected.

Your walk with God becomes hollow, because you're always performing and never surrendering.

And worst of all—your legacy becomes unintentionally broken.

Why? Because what you fail to own now, your children will have to heal from later.

The Responsibility You Can't Delegate

You can hire someone to clean your house.

You can pay someone to fix your roof.

You can appoint leaders to run your business.

But no one else can:

Apologize for the words you said.

Heal the relationships you broke.

Lead your children into spiritual truth.

Step up and be the man God called you to be.

This assignment is yours.

The Four Levels of Ownership

1. Personal Responsibility

Own your attitude. Own your decisions. Own your time. Don't just be busy—be purposeful.

Ask:

"Did I act out of fear or faith today?"

"Did I give my best, or just do enough?"

2. Relational Responsibility

Relationships don't thrive on presence alone—they thrive on emotional investment.

Ask:

"Have I made those around me feel safe or shut down?"

"Have I apologized when I've been wrong—even when it hurt my pride?"

3. Spiritual Responsibility

Your wife shouldn't be the only one praying.

Your children shouldn't have to wonder what you believe.

Your church shouldn't be the only place you act spiritual.

Ask:

"Have I asked God today to order my steps?"

"Am I spiritually covering what I complain about?"

4. Generational Responsibility

You're building a culture in your family with every decision you make.

Ask:

"What will my grandchildren inherit because of the stand I take today?"

"What dysfunction ends with me?"

"What faith begins with me?"

Field Notes: One Text That Changed Everything

A middle-aged father once came to me and said, *"My son hasn't talked to me in months. I know I messed up. I just don't know how to fix it."*

I told him: *"Start with a text. Just own it."*

He wrote: *"Son, I don't expect you to forget. But I want to say I was wrong. I should've done better. And if you're open, I want to try again."*

The next day, his son responded.

Two weeks later, they had dinner.

Months later, the son said,

"You didn't become perfect—but you became real. And that's what I needed."

Responsibility creates connection.

Not by being flawless—but by being honest, available, and committed.

Scripture Foundation

"He that is faithful in that which is least is faithful also in much..." – **Luke 16:10**

"Be watchful, stand fast in the faith, quit you like men, be strong." – **1 Corinthians 16:13**

"He that covereth his sins shall not prosper: but whoso confesseth and forsaketh them shall have mercy." – **Proverbs 28:13**

"The just man walketh in his integrity: his children are blessed after him." – **Proverbs 20:7**

Reflection Questions

What part of your life are you managing instead of owning?

Who around you is quietly carrying the weight of something you should've handled?

What healing could start if you simply said, *"I was wrong"* or *"I didn't show up when I should have"?*

What legacy do you want to leave—and what part of that starts with taking responsibility today?

Prayer of Full Responsibility

Heavenly Father, I bring You every place where I've ignored truth, shifted blame, or buried what should have been addressed. I repent for what I've avoided and for who I've hurt in the process. I ask You for the strength to take full responsibility—not just in words, but in action. Give me wisdom. Give me humility. Help me restore what I've broken, protect what You've entrusted to me, and honor You with how I lead. I take ownership of my life, my household, and my future. In Jesus' name, amen.

Chapter 7

The Stand-Up Man in the Community

"Ye are the light of the world. A city that is set on an hill cannot be hid." – **Matthew 5:14 (KJV)**

Not Just in the Home—But in the Hood, the Halls, and the Hedges

A true man doesn't stop leading at the edge of his driveway.

His influence travels—because his presence speaks.

He shows up at home with faith.

He shows up at church with commitment.

He shows up in the workplace with discipline.

And he shows up in the community with purpose.

Today's world doesn't just need more programs.

It needs more men—in position, on assignment, and unafraid to say:

"This is my neighborhood. These are my people. And I will not stay silent."

When men stand up in the community, everything starts to shift.

What Happens When Men Disappear from the Streets

We've seen the headlines.

We've walked past the memorials.

We've heard the cries of single mothers, broken schools, overburdened churches, and ignored youth.

It's not always about crime—it's about absence.

When righteous men pull back, darkness fills the void.

False role models rise.

Generational curses cycle again.

Communities operate in survival mode.

Local politics drift without accountability.

Neighborhood culture becomes loud, reckless, and spiritually dull.

Satan doesn't need to destroy men. He just needs them distracted, disqualified, or disengaged.

A City on a Hill Cannot Be Hidden

Jesus didn't say, *"Try to be the light."*

He said, *"You are the light."*

You don't need a stage, a mic, or a title.

You just need presence and purity.

You're called to stand where others fall.

To build where others break down.

To bless where others curse.

To shine where others shut down.

The Stand-Up Man doesn't hide behind his house.

He walks the community with confidence—not in himself, but in the God who called him.

Five Places the Stand-Up Man Is Needed

1. The School

The classroom is a battleground of identity.

Young people walk in carrying:

father wounds,

emotional trauma,

and questions no one is answering.

What if your presence was the answer?

When men volunteer at schools:

Discipline improves.

Respect returns.

Students feel covered.

The standard rises.

Whether it's mentoring during lunch, greeting at the door, or praying over the property—you matter in the hallways.

2. The Church

The church is not just a building. It's a training ground. A launchpad.

If men stay on the sidelines:

Worship becomes weak.

Prayer becomes one-sided.

The next generation grows up unsure if God is for them—because men of God are absent.

Real men:

Lift their hands in worship.

Cry before the Lord.

Correct in love.

Teach the Word.

Serve without needing thanks.

Your church doesn't need your opinion—it needs your presence and your obedience.

3. The Barbershop

This is where culture is shaped in casual conversation. Laughter flows. Truth surfaces. Opinions spark.

But when the Stand-Up Man sits in the chair:

Gossip gets redirected.

Ignorance gets corrected.

God gets mentioned.

Wisdom is dropped without a lecture.

You don't have to dominate the room.

Just drop seeds. Be salt. Be real. And be rooted.

4. The Corner Store, The Court, and The Corner

Your community doesn't need superheroes.

It needs familiar, faithful, steady men.

That means:

Dapping up the teens who never hear *"I'm proud of you."*

Supporting the coach with your time, not just your talk.

Speaking peace in parking lots where arguments begin.

Making your face familiar to young boys who don't know what safety feels like.

You become known—and your presence begins to carry weight.

5. City Halls, School Boards, and Civic Spaces

Policy is shaped in rooms most men ignore.

But the Stand-Up Man doesn't wait until something goes wrong—he shows up early and speaks up often.

Don't let decisions be made about your community without your insight, your prayers, or your conviction in the room.

We need men who:

Read what's on the ballot.

Show up to hearings.

Ask questions that matter.

Represent the Kingdom with clarity and courage.

Field Notes: The Shift One Man Created

In a struggling neighborhood, a retired mechanic began mentoring boys on his front porch.

He didn't have a title, a grant, or a pulpit.

Just a picnic table, a Bible, some tools, and time.

He called it *"Manhood Mondays."*

Every week, 6 to 10 young men came.

They learned to:

Knot ties.

Change oil.

Pray over their future.

Say ***"Yes, sir"*** and ***"No, ma'am."***

Shake hands with dignity.

That neighborhood still had problems—but those boys? They stood taller. Talked differently. Walked with purpose.

Because one man stood up.

Scripture Foundation

"And I sought for a man among them, that should make up the hedge, and stand in the gap..." – **Ezekiel 22:30 (KJV)**

"Watch ye, stand fast in the faith, quit you like men, be strong." – **1 Corinthians 16:13 (KJV)**

"Let your light so shine before men..." – **Matthew 5:16 (KJV)**

"They looked unto him, and were lightened: and their faces were not ashamed." – **Psalm 34:5 (KJV)**

Reflection Questions

Where is God asking me to show up—but I've stayed silent or distant?

What group of young men or families could benefit from my wisdom, presence, or prayers?

Have I allowed fear, busyness, or past hurt to keep me from walking in public purpose?

What one action can I take this week to stand up beyond my house?

Prayer of Community Covering

Lord, give me vision for more than my own house. Break my heart for what breaks Yours in my community. Let me be a light—firm but gentle, bold but humble, clear but compassionate. I repent for being passive. I receive Your courage to stand at the gates, walk the streets, and speak life into dry places. Use me to protect, guide, restore, and bless my city—not through pride, but through presence. In Jesus' name, amen.

Chapter 8

Standing in the Face of Pressure

"Watch ye, stand fast in the faith, quit you like men, be strong." – 1 Corinthians 16:13 (KJV)

The Pressure Is Real—and So Is Your Purpose

If you've ever stood at the edge of a breakdown with no words left to pray…

If you've ever looked in the mirror and wondered how long you can keep pretending to be strong…

If you've ever felt the weight of being the provider, protector, peacemaker, and problem-solver—all while fighting your own private battles…

You're not alone.

Pressure is the invisible force pushing against every man who dares to rise.

And the truth is: the greater the purpose, the heavier the pressure.

You were never promised ease. But you were promised strength.

Not a strength that comes from muscles or money—but from being rooted in something deeper.

God never called you to carry it all alone—He called you to carry it with Him.

Understanding the Layers of Pressure

Pressure is more than stress. It's the invisible weight of responsibility paired with the internal expectation of perfection.
It's what makes men grind in silence and collapse in private.

Pressure isn't always about the obvious—it hides in layers:

Silent pressure – When no one checks in because they think you're okay.

Inherited pressure – When you're trying to fix what generations before you never got right.

Performative pressure – When you feel like failure isn't allowed and authenticity is too risky.

Spiritual pressure – When the closer you get to God, the more the enemy comes for your focus.

Pressure, when not processed properly, turns warriors into wanderers.

But when faced with faith and truth—it turns broken men into bold ones.

Pressure Has Purpose—but It Also Has a Pattern

Pressure doesn't just arrive randomly—it follows movement.
When you start standing for righteousness, expect resistance.

Joseph stood in integrity—he got thrown into prison.

Moses stood in leadership—he was crushed by the weight of complaining people.

Jesus stood in purpose—He was betrayed, beaten, crucified.

But none of them stayed down.

Because pressure is not the end—it's the proving ground.
What's forming in the fire will be stronger than what ever lived in the comfort zone.

The Real Voice of Pressure

Pressure often speaks in disguise:

"You're the problem."

"You're never going to be enough."

"You better not ask for help."

"You'll lose everything if you show weakness."

And here's what most men have been trained to do:

Power through silently.

Show up anyway—wounded and unwell.

Smile in public and suffer in private.

Numb it with distractions—food, sex, work, social media, even ministry.

But what if pressure is not meant to crush you—but to crack open the shell of who you used to be?

Field Notes: A Man Who Almost Quit

A business owner. Husband. Father of three.
Highly respected in his church and admired in his community.

One day he said to me, **"I'**ve planned my exit. I love my family—but I don't know who I am when I'm not performing for them."

The pressure had built over years—expectations he never challenged, emotions he never released, pain he never confessed.

He wasn't a bad man. He was a burdened one.

Through prayer, mentorship, honest counseling, and support from his brothers, he found his voice again.

He didn't just survive the pressure.

He re-emerged stronger, softer, more secure.

And now? He mentors men who almost gave up like he did.

That's the power of standing—especially when you feel like sinking.

How Do You Stand When Everything Feels Heavy?

1. Acknowledge the Weight Without Shame

It's okay to say:

"I'm tired."

"I feel overwhelmed."

"I'm carrying too much."

God never blesses the mask. He blesses the man willing to be real.

2. Anchor Yourself in God's Promises

Pressure tries to pull you into your emotions.
God pulls you back into truth.

"When my heart is overwhelmed: lead me to the rock that is higher than I." – **Psalm 61:2 (KJV)**

Make Scripture your foundation—not your fallback.

3. Pray Raw Prayers

Not polished. Not perfect. Just real.

God already knows what you're feeling.

The goal is not performance—it's presence.

4. Create a Safety Circle

You weren't made to stand alone.

Who knows the real you?

Who checks in when you're quiet?

Who holds your arms up when you're tired?

Every strong man has someone holding him up behind the scenes.

5. Pause When Necessary—But Never Quit

Rest isn't weakness.

Silence isn't surrender.

A pause is not a failure.

Take a break. Breathe. Step back. But then stand again.

Scripture Foundation

"Be not weary in well doing: for in due season we shall reap, if we faint not." – **Galatians 6:9 (KJV)**

"Many are the afflictions of the righteous: but the Lord delivereth him out of them all." – **Psalm 34:19 (KJV)**

"But the God of all grace… after that ye have suffered a while, make you perfect, stablish, strengthen, settle you." – **1 Peter 5:10 (KJV)**

"Cast thy burden upon the Lord, and he shall sustain thee…" – **Psalm 55:22 (KJV)**

Reflection Questions

What are the specific pressures you're currently carrying? Name them honestly.

How have you been coping? Healthy or hidden?

What part of your faith are you struggling to believe under this pressure?

Who can help you carry this—without judgment, but with truth?

What would happen if you stood one more day?

Prayer of Endurance and Expectation

Father, I feel the pressure. The silent strain. The fatigue in my soul. But I choose to stand—not because I feel strong, but because You are my strength. Teach me to breathe when the burden builds. Teach me to lean when I want to run. Remind me that I don't carry this alone. Give me the courage to keep showing up, the wisdom to set boundaries, and the faith to trust You with outcomes I can't control. This pressure won't break me—it will build me. In Jesus' name, ***amen.***

Chapter 9

The Power of Consistency

"Moreover it is required in stewards, that a man be found faithful." – 1 Corinthians 4:2 (KJV)

Consistency Is the Crown of the Mature Man

Consistency is not sexy. It doesn't trend.

It rarely gets thanked.

But it builds trust, legacy, and power like nothing else.

You don't have to be loud to be legendary.

You just have to be steady when it matters most.

Anybody can show up when it's exciting.

Anybody can promise change when emotions are high.

Anybody can start something new when the energy is fresh.

But the Stand-Up Man keeps showing up:

When it's hard.

When it's boring.

When he feels unseen.

When it would be easier to walk away.

Because he knows faithfulness isn't optional. It's foundational.

The Psychology of Consistency: What Happens When You Keep Showing Up

Consistency reprograms your mind. It moves you:

From excuses to execution.

From ambition to actual growth.

From self-doubt to self-discipline.

From chaos to character.

Most men want change.

But they haven't developed the rhythm to support it.

You don't rise to the level of your intentions. You fall to the level of your habits.

Consistency is proof you take yourself seriously.

Why Inconsistency Is So Destructive

Inconsistency sends mixed signals to the people around you—and to the God who's assigned you.

Your spouse wonders if you're serious.

Your kids begin to internalize your absence.

Your dreams lose momentum.

Your faith stagnates.

Your anointing becomes dormant.

Inconsistent men don't fail all at once.

They erode decision by decision, break by break, missed day by missed day.

And then they wake up wondering how they drifted so far from who they said they'd be.

The Long-Term Power of Doing the Right Thing Daily

Let's be clear:

Reading one verse won't change your life. Reading the Word daily will.

Saying *"I love you"* once won't fix a relationship. Saying it with action every day builds safety.

Praying once won't break a curse. Praying consistently can rewrite your legacy.

One workout won't fix your health. Discipline will.

God honors the mundane done with maturity.

He builds strong men in the quiet repetition of:

Integrity

Obedience

Self-control

Sacrifice

And if you do it long enough, your consistency will outlive your excuses.

Field Notes: The Man Who Never Stopped Coming Back

A man once told me:

"I never feel like I'm the best at anything. But I'm always willing to be the most consistent in the room."

He lost jobs—but kept showing up.

He battled depression—but kept praying.

He got overlooked—but kept learning.

He was misunderstood—but kept loving.

And now?

His life is full of the fruit of what others abandoned.

Not because he had it all together—but because he didn't stop.

Five Areas Where Consistency Matters Most

1. Your Walk with God

The strongest men spiritually aren't always the ones who shout the loudest.

They're the ones who:

Read when it's dry

Worship when it's tough

Pray when it's quiet

Trust when it's dark

They don't just seek God in storms.

They walk with Him in silence.

2. Your Integrity

Be the same man:

In public and in private

In pressure and in peace

When no one's watching

Your name becomes your credibility.

And credibility is the currency of manhood.

3. Your Family

Your wife needs consistency more than charisma.

Your children need daily attention more than weekend gifts.

The presence you maintain becomes the security they carry.

Consistency in tone. Consistency in love. Consistency in correction.

That's what produces emotionally whole families.

4. Your Leadership

Great leaders don't always innovate.

But they always follow through.

Whether you're leading a team, a ministry, or your household:

Keep showing up to the hard conversations

Keep making the right decisions

Keep modeling what matters

Leaders lead by example, not announcement.

5. Your Health—Physical, Mental, Emotional

Your body is a temple.

Your mind is a battlefield.

Your emotions are part of your humanity—not your enemy.

If you neglect your health inconsistently, you will collapse eventually.

Stretch.

Rest.

Pray.

Eat well.

Get therapy if needed.

Say **"no"** when overloaded.

Journal your thoughts.

Small, repeated steps protect great callings.

Scripture Foundation

"He that is faithful in that which is least is faithful also in much..." – **Luke 16:10 (KJV)**

"Let us not be weary in well doing: for in due season we shall reap, if we faint not." – **Galatians 6:9 (KJV)**

"The just man walketh in his integrity: his children are blessed after him." – **Proverbs 20:7 (KJV)**

"If ye continue in my word, then are ye my disciples indeed." – **John 8:31 (KJV)**

Reflection & Activation

What area of your life has suffered most because of inconsistency?

What excuses have you used to justify stopping, quitting, or pausing too often?

Who in your life has been affected by your inconsistency—and how can you make it right?

What's one small thing you can commit to doing daily that would produce long-term impact?

What would change in 6 months if you stayed steady, even in the shadows?

Prayer of Daily Faithfulness

Lord, I've started many things. I've made promises. I've wanted to grow. But I confess—I've often lacked consistency. I repent for breaking rhythm, losing discipline, and relying too much on moments. Teach me to build with my habits. Show me how to honor You with my daily choices. Make me a steady man. A man whose faith stands in silence, whose words match his walk, and whose life leaves a trail of truth. I commit to show up, even when it's hard. I commit to be faithful, even when I'm not seen. Make consistency my legacy. In Jesus' name, amen.

Chapter 10

How Men Restore What Was Broken

"And they that shall be of thee shall build the old waste places: thou shalt raise up the foundations of many generations; and thou shalt be called, The repairer of the breach, The restorer of paths to dwell in." – **Isaiah 58:12 (KJV)**

God Still Uses Broken Men to Rebuild Broken Places

Every man has stood among ruins at some point in his life.

A shattered relationship

A scarred reputation

A fractured family

A spiritual collapse

An abandoned calling

But God doesn't discard broken men—He recruits them for restoration.

You may have messed up.

You may have walked away.

You may have stayed silent when you should've spoken, or spoken when you should've stayed silent.

Still, God calls you to rebuild.

Not because you're perfect—but because you're willing.

Restoration doesn't require applause.

It requires a man who says:

"This time, I'm doing the work. This time, I'm not walking away. This time, I'm rebuilding what I once broke."

What Does It Mean to Restore?

To restore doesn't mean to go back.

It means to build something stronger in the same place where something once fell.

Restoration isn't fixing—it's renewing.

It means:

Owning the damage

Embracing the process

Repairing with integrity

Working without guarantee of recognition

Loving even if the results are slow

It's spiritual construction with emotional and relational tools.

The Weight and Worth of Restoration

Restoration is hard because:

It takes time

It requires humility

It costs your pride

It confronts your failures

It demands forgiveness—both giving and receiving

But it's worth it because:

It heals what trauma tried to own

It reclaims what sin tried to stain

It releases peace to those you once hurt

It reroutes the next generation

You don't just rebuild for you—you rebuild for them. Your children. Your spouse. Your community. Your legacy.

Field Notes: A Son's Journal

A young man wrote this in his journal:

"I don't hate my dad. I just wish he knew what he missed. I needed him to show up. To listen. To guide. To admit he was wrong sometimes."

Years later, his father found the journal.

He wept.

Then he repented.

He didn't try to defend himself—he simply called and said:

"I found your words. And I don't want to be the same man who caused them."

From that day forward, the father began restoring— through presence, prayer, and persistence.

Five Stages of True Restoration

1. Revelation: See What's Broken

Ask yourself:

What relationship or space did I walk away from?

What pain did I ignore?

What promise did I break?

What wounds are unspoken?

You can't restore what you won't recognize.

2. Responsibility: Own It Without Excuse

Say things like:

"That was my fault."

"You were right—I shut down."

"I blamed you when I should've helped you."

Don't wait to feel ready.

Take responsibility anyway.

3. Repentance: Turn in a New Direction

Repentance isn't just confession—it's course correction.

It means:

Apologizing with sincerity

Asking for nothing in return

Seeking healing, not just harmony

Walking in a new rhythm—not repeating cycles

4. Rebuilding: Start Small, Stay Consistent

Rebuilding doesn't begin with grand gestures.

It begins with:

Returned phone calls

Kept promises

Steady communication

Showing up even when you're not sure if they'll receive you

Restoration is earned daily through humility and faithfulness.

5. Renewal: Let God Finish What You Started

Some wounds are beyond your repair.

That's where God steps in.

Pray:

"Lord, do the heart work I cannot reach. Heal what my words can't fix. Strengthen what my hands can't hold. Finish what I've started."

What Happens When Men Restore

1. Homes Heal

When a man becomes the repairer of the breach:

Communication reopens.

Trust is reintroduced.

Children find stability.

Wives feel safe again.

2. Hearts Heal

Restoration brings:

Emotional release

Mental peace

Spiritual growth

Permission to forgive

You stop the bleeding—not just for others, but within yourself.

3. Generations Heal

What you fix now becomes:

Your children's emotional framework

Your grandchildren's relational baseline

Your community's testimony of hope

You don't just restore for today.

You restore for decades to come.

Scripture Foundation

"I will restore health unto thee, and I will heal thee of thy wounds, saith the Lord..." – **Jeremiah 30:17 (KJV)**

"Brethren, if a man be overtaken in a fault, ye which are spiritual, restore such an one in the spirit of meekness..." – **Galatians 6:1 (KJV)**

"He healeth the broken in heart, and bindeth up their wounds." – Psalm 147:3 (KJV)

"Create in me a clean heart, O God; and renew a right spirit within me." – **Psalm 51:10 (KJV)**

"For I will restore health unto thee, and I will heal thee of thy wounds..." – **Jeremiah 30:17 (KJV)**

Reflection & Activation

What area of your life still bears the cracks of something you broke?

Have you truly owned your part—or just explained it away?

What small step could you take this week to begin rebuilding trust?

Who needs to hear from you—not to fix everything, but to know you're ready to do the work?

Are you willing to be consistent, even if the restoration journey is long and slow?

Prayer of Restoration and Renewal

Lord, I bring every broken place to You—what I caused, what I ignored, what I didn't know how to fix. I confess my pride, my silence, my absence. Teach me to rebuild what I once tore down. Guide me as I seek to restore trust, to ask for forgiveness, to repair relationships. Help me show up with consistency and grace. Use my hands to rebuild what sin tried to destroy. And let my life be a testimony that nothing is too far gone for You to heal. In Jesus' name, amen.

Chapter 11

When Men Pray

"I will therefore that men pray every where, lifting up holy hands, without wrath and doubting." **– 1 Timothy 2:8 (KJV)**

A Man's Posture Before God Shapes His Power Before Men

Prayer is not passive.

Prayer is not soft.

Prayer is not weak.

Prayer is warfare.

Prayer is alignment.

Prayer is intimacy with the Creator of the universe.

When men pray:

Cycles are broken

Atmospheres shift

Children are covered

Marriages are fortified

Strategies are revealed

Demons are resisted

Generations are changed

You don't need a title to be effective in prayer.
You just need a surrendered spirit and a willing mouth.

What Prayer Does to a Man

Prayer does more than change things—it changes the man praying.

1. It softens his heart.

Prayer breaks pride, melts anger, and heals bitterness.

2. It sharpens his focus.

Distractions fade when you're tuned into heaven.

3. It steadies his emotions.

Prayer calms storms that rage in the mind and soul.

4. It strengthens his identity.

You stop praying like a beggar and start praying like a beloved son.

5. It sets spiritual order.

When a man takes his place in prayer, everything else begins to fall into place.

Field Notes: The Man Who Took the Role Back

There was a man who had been passive for years.
His wife was the spiritual leader of the house.
His kids saw her pray, worship, fast, and cover them.
He was a good man—but he was spiritually quiet.

Until one day, his son came home angry from school and slammed the door.

His wife went to speak, but this time—the father stepped forward.

He walked into the room, laid his hands on the door, and prayed:

"Lord, whatever is attacking my son's mind, silence it now. Fill this room with Your peace. Let him know he's not fighting alone. I take spiritual responsibility—starting now."

That wasn't just a moment—it was a transfer of authority.

From then on, that man prayed first thing in the morning and last thing at night.

And the culture of his home began to shift.

Why? Because a man stood up—on his knees.

When Men Pray, Legacies Shift

Strongholds Are Broken

Addictions begin to unravel

Bitterness begins to dissolve

Cycles of dysfunction begin to crumble

Homes Are Protected

You're not just locking doors at night—you're sealing your house in prayer.

Minds Are Renewed

Anxious thoughts bow to the peace of God.

Sudden clarity replaces prolonged confusion.

Seeds Are Planted in Children

Even if your kids don't say it—they notice when you pray.

And when they're grown, they'll remember, *"My father prayed."*

How to Establish a Prayer Life That Lasts

1. Make It a Non-Negotiable

Schedule your time with God like you would a business meeting or a doctor's appointment.

Morning: *"God, lead my day."*

Noon: *"God, keep my focus."*

Night: *"God, thank You for keeping me."*

2. Designate Your Space

You don't need a war room.

Just a consistent place—your car, a corner, a closet, your kitchen table.

When your space becomes sacred, your time becomes supernatural.

3. Pray with Expectation

Don't just talk. Listen. Expect. Record. Obey.

Ask, and it shall be given. Seek, and ye shall find. **(Matthew 7:7)**

4. Pray with Authority

Stop begging for what God already gave you access to.

Declare peace over your mind

Speak life over your family

Bind confusion

Loose joy

Call out destiny

You are not just requesting—you're releasing.

5. Model It Out Loud

Pray where your wife can hear you.

Pray where your children can see you.

Let them know that God is not just someone you believe in—but someone you talk to.

Scripture Foundation

"The effectual fervent prayer of a righteous man availeth much." – **James 5:16 (KJV)**

"Watch ye and pray, lest ye enter into temptation." – **Mark 14:38 (KJV)**

"Call unto me, and I will answer thee, and show thee great and mighty things…" – **Jeremiah 33:3 (KJV)**

"Likewise the Spirit also helpeth our infirmities… the Spirit itself maketh intercession for us…" – **Romans 8:26 (KJV)**

"Is any among you afflicted? let him pray…" – **James 5:13 (KJV)**

Reflection Questions

1. Have I neglected my position as the spiritual covering of my home through silence or inconsistency in prayer?

2. What has God been waiting for me to talk to Him about?

3. What strongholds or struggles in my life could begin to break if I committed to a consistent prayer life?

4. Who in my life is silently depending on me to stand in the gap?

5. What would shift in my family, workplace, or city if I made prayer my first response instead of my last resort?

A Man's Prayer of Alignment

Father, thank You for reminding me that I don't have to be perfect to pray—I just have to be present. I step into my rightful place as a praying man. I choose to speak life. I choose to cover my home. I choose to intercede for those around me. Where I've been silent, wake up my voice. Where I've been passive, reignite my fire. Teach me to pray with power, listen with humility, and walk with confidence. Let my life reflect heaven—and let my prayers open doors that no man can shut. In Jesus' name, amen.

Chapter 12

When Men Forgive

"And be ye kind one to another, tenderhearted, forgiving one another, even as God for Christ's sake hath forgiven you." – **Ephesians 4:32 (KJV)**

Forgiveness Isn't a Feeling—It's a Fight for Freedom

Some men never forgive—not because they're cold, but because they were never taught how.

They confuse forgiveness with weakness, or they believe forgiveness means they *"lost."*

But here's the truth:

The man who forgives isn't losing anything—he's regaining everything.

His voice

His peace

His sleep

His joy

His ability to love

His future

Forgiveness is not denial.

It's not erasure.

It's a decision to stop bleeding over moments you can't change.

When a man forgives, he steps out of the shadows of pain and back into the light of purpose.

The Unseen Toll of Unforgiveness on a Man's Life

Unforgiveness doesn't sit quietly in a corner.

It invades every room of your life.

It clouds your vision.

You start seeing every new relationship through the lens of past betrayal.

It affects your thinking.

You replay the wrong. You second-guess trust. You anticipate rejection.

It warps your words.

Sarcasm becomes armor. Silence becomes punishment. Conversations become confrontations. It hardens your heart.

You mistake numbness for strength. You protect yourself from pain—but also from love.

It holds your calling hostage.

You can't lead boldly while emotionally stuck in yesterday's prison.

Some men don't need more motivation.

They need emotional release through forgiveness.

Field Notes: The Leader Who Carried Bitterness in Silence

He was admired. Respected. Looked up to.

But inside?

He was angry. Not wild anger—but quiet resentment.

His father had walked out.

His ex-wife had cheated.

His former mentor had betrayed his trust.

He told me:

"I forgive—but I'll never forget."

But his eyes said otherwise.

His tone said otherwise.

His heart had walls.

His faith had fatigue.

One day, I asked, *"What if you're not called to forget— but to finally let it go?"*

Tears welled up. That day, he broke.

He wept. He released. He forgave—not for them, but for himself.

He later said:

"That was the first time I prayed without resentment in ten years."

Forgiveness didn't change what happened.

It changed him.

Four Myths That Keep Men from Forgiving

1. *"If I forgive, they win."*

No—they don't. You win.

You win your peace, your presence, and your power back.

2. *"If I forgive, it means I was weak."*

Forgiveness doesn't make you weak.

It proves you're strong enough to carry grace instead of grudge.

3. *"They don't deserve it."*

Maybe not. But neither did we when Christ forgave us.

4. "It won't make a difference."

It will. Maybe not to them. But to you? It could heal everything.

The Forgiveness Process: Five Stages to Begin Healing

1. Honesty

Don't downplay the pain.

Admit:

"That hurt."

"They broke something in me."

"I'm still mad, still sad, still confused."

God won't heal what we won't acknowledge.

2. Responsibility

You may not be responsible for what happened.

But you are responsible for what you carry next.

3. Release

Say it aloud:

"I forgive them. Not because they asked. Not because they changed. But because I choose to be free."

Forgiveness is a gift you give yourself.

4. Reframe

You're not the victim anymore. You're the overcomer.

The pain helped you grow. It deepened your wisdom. It opened your compassion.

5. Repeat

Forgiveness is not always a one-time event.

Sometimes you have to keep releasing until the wound stops bleeding.

Who Needs Your Forgiveness?

The Father Who Wasn't There

You've carried the weight of his absence long enough.
Release the resentment, and be the man he never learned how to be.

The Ex Who Wounded You

You loved them. They left—or betrayed you.
Let it go. The rest of your life doesn't belong to a past chapter.

The Friend Who Switched Up

Don't let their disloyalty become your new standard of distrust.
Learn the lesson, but keep your heart open.

Yourself

For all the times you blew it, missed it, ignored it.
God already forgave you. Now it's your turn.

Scripture Foundation

"Forgive, and ye shall be forgiven." – **Luke 6:37 (KJV)**

"Create in me a clean heart, O God..." – **Psalm 51:10 (KJV)**

"Let all bitterness... and evil speaking, be put away from you..." – **Ephesians 4:31 (KJV)**

"Love covers a multitude of sins." – **1 Peter 4:8 (KJV)**

"Blessed are the pure in heart: for they shall see God." – **Matthew 5:8 (KJV)**

Reflection & Activation

1. What name, memory, or event still causes an emotional reaction in you?

2. What would emotional peace feel like if you no longer carried that grudge?

3. Have you confused *"moving on"* with actually forgiving?

4. What apologies are you still waiting on—and what's stopping you from forgiving without them?

5. What version of yourself would be unlocked if you forgave fully?

Prayer of Liberation Through Forgiveness

Father, I release every weight I've carried. The betrayal. The silence. The abandonment. The anger. I forgive them—not because they earned it, but because I refuse to be controlled by pain. I forgive myself—for mistakes I made, for time I wasted, for what I didn't know back then. I forgive the people who should've loved me better. I release the judgment I've held in my heart. Fill the empty places with peace, with grace, and with a heart that loves without fear. I won't carry what You've already taken. In Jesus' name, amen.

Chapter 13

When Men Confront the Mirror

The Honest Look That Leads to Lasting Change

"Examine me, O Lord, and prove me; try my reins and my heart." – **Psalm 26:2 (KJV)**

The Mirror Shows What the Mask Hides

Every man has a moment where the crowd is gone, the noise fades, and the spotlight turns inward.

It's just him and the mirror.

Not the physical mirror in his bathroom—but the spiritual mirror God uses to reveal:

What's beneath the surface

What's behind the anger

What's under the control

What's left unspoken

This moment isn't about guilt. It's about growth.

When a man finally stops blaming others and bravely confronts what's going on inside, everything changes.

The mirror won't lie to you.

The question is—will you listen to what it shows?

What the Mirror Might Reveal

When you really look, you might see:

A husband who never healed from rejection

A father repeating patterns he swore to break

A leader more insecure than he appears

A believer going through the motions

A man stuck in survival mode while calling it "strength"

Confronting the mirror hurts—but what hurts can also heal.

Field Notes: A Pastor, a Mirror, and a Moment of Truth

He had built a ministry, preached hope, and served faithfully.

But after years of silent burnout, hidden disappointment, and self-neglect, the Lord whispered:

"You've helped many find Me—but when will you let Me fully restore you?"

He wept in his office alone.

Not because of scandal, sin, or shame.

But because he saw himself clearly for the first time in years.

And that was the beginning of a deeper surrender.

Five Things Men Must Learn to Recognize in the Mirror

1. Unspoken Wounds

Some pain has no language.

But unaddressed trauma will always express itself— through anger, silence, or overcompensation.

Healing starts when you name what hurt you.

2. Emotional Numbness

You're functioning… but are you feeling?
You show up… but are you present?

Emotional suppression is not emotional strength.

3. False Strength

You're not *"strong"* if you never cry, never share, and never rest.

You're just numb with armor on.

Real strength is measured in transparency, not toughness.

4. Compromised Conviction

What used to bother you, doesn't anymore.
You've normalized spiritual drift.

The mirror doesn't just show where you fell—it shows where you started slipping.

5. Buried Purpose

The man you were born to be is still buried under fear, fatigue, and forgotten dreams.

Looking in the mirror might just reintroduce you to the man God called—not just the man life shaped.

How to Respond When the Mirror Speaks

Step 1: Stop Justifying

Let go of:

"That's just how I am."

"They pushed me there."

"I've always struggled with this."

Excuses keep you stuck. Responsibility sets you free.

Step 2: Confess Out Loud

Don't just think it. Speak it.

Let God and a trusted brother hear what you've hidden.

"I'm tired."

"I'm broken in this area."

"I've been slipping."

"I need help."

Step 3: Invite Accountability

Don't just glance at the mirror once.

Build a life where the mirror is a regular part of your rhythm.

Let someone check your:

Attitude

Habits

Spiritual temperature

Emotional honesty

The man who walks with no accountability is headed toward quiet collapse.

Step 4: Commit to Change, Not Just Clarity

It's one thing to see the truth. It's another to act on it.

Make one decision today:

Counseling

Rest

Repentance

A phone call

A re-commitment

A new routine

Scripture Foundation

"For if any be a hearer of the word, and not a doer, he is like unto a man beholding his natural face in a glass..." **– James 1:23 (KJV)**

"The heart is deceitful above all things, and desperately wicked: who can know it?" **– Jeremiah 17:9 (KJV)**

"Create in me a clean heart, O God; and renew a right spirit within me." – **Psalm 51:10 (KJV)**

"Faithful are the wounds of a friend…" – **Proverbs 27:6 (KJV)**

Reflection Questions

1. When was the last time I stopped and truly examined my heart?

2. What am I pretending doesn't exist—emotionally, spiritually, or relationally?

3. What would change if I told the truth about where I really am?

4. Who is one trusted person I can bring into this journey of self-examination?

5. What is the mirror showing me right now—and what am I going to do about it?

A Man's Prayer at the Mirror

Lord, I stand before You with no mask, no defense, and no excuses. Search me. Reveal what I've ignored. Shine light into what I've kept in the dark. Help me not just see—but surrender. Not just confess—but change. Let this be the moment I return to You fully—with honesty,

hunger, and humility. Make me whole again. In Jesus'
name, amen.

Chapter 14

When Men Rebuild What Was Broken

From Confession to Construction

"And they that shall be of thee shall build the old waste places: thou shalt raise up the foundations of many generations..." – **Isaiah 58:12 (KJV)**

From Wreckage to Restoration

There's a moment after repentance where many men feel stuck.

They've confessed. They've cried

They've acknowledged their wrongs.

Now what?

Now… you rebuild.

You pick up the shovel.

You gather the stones.

You roll up your sleeves.

You build again—with grace, truth, humility, and consistency.

Rebuilding is where real change begins.

It's where emotional awareness becomes action.
Where inner conviction becomes visible transformation.
And where what was once lost can now become a testimony of restoration.

Why Rebuilding Is Hard—but Holy

Rebuilding isn't about control—it's about character.

It's not about *"getting things back."*

It's about becoming the kind of man who can handle what God is ready to trust you with next.

That means:

Rebuilding trust with people you hurt

Rebuilding routines that promote health

Rebuilding faith where disappointment lived

Rebuilding courage to lead again after failure

Rebuilding your name—not for pride, but for testimony

"Let integrity and uprightness preserve me..." – **Psalm 25:21**

Field Notes: The Husband Who Rebuilt His Role

I met a man who confessed to neglecting his wife emotionally for over a decade.

She was still in the house—but the connection was gone.

After he repented and confronted himself, he began to rebuild.

Not with flowers or grand speeches—but with:

A changed tone

Prayer at the dinner table

Helping with things he used to ignore

Listening without interrupting

Making time, not just giving money

Following through on promises

Six months later, she said:

"You're not the man I married. You're the man I prayed he would become."

Rebuilding is slow, but it's sacred.

Rebuilding Requires Four Commitments

1. Commit to Showing Up Even When You Don't Feel It

Rebuilders don't wait for motivation—they move in obedience.

Show up to the conversation.

Show up to the counseling session.

Show up in prayer.

Show up for the hard talk with your child.

Show up with service, not just words.

2. Commit to Relearning What You Thought You Knew

You can't rebuild with old blueprints.

This season will require:

New language

New rhythms

New levels of patience

New spiritual disciplines

Don't say, *"This is just how I've always been."*

Say, *"God, teach me how to build right this time."*

3. Commit to Grace-Based Growth, Not Perfection

You will make mistakes. You will fall short. You may be misunderstood.

But don't quit.

Your consistency will begin to echo louder than your past.

"They may not trust your words yet—but let them learn to trust your walk."

4. Commit to God's Process Over Your Deadline

You may want things fixed by Friday.

God may be rebuilding your character over the next year.

Trust the slow work of the Spirit.

Ask:

"Lord, what are You forming in me during this time?"

"Who am I becoming—not just what am I fixing?"

What Rebuilt Men Do Differently

They apologize without expectation.

They honor without needing recognition.

They forgive before being asked.

They show up without needing applause.

They set boundaries, build habits, and lead with healing—not ego.

Scripture Foundation

"Except the Lord build the house, they labour in vain that build it…" – **Psalm 127:1 (KJV)**

"If a man purge himself… he shall be a vessel unto honour, sanctified, and meet for the master's use…" – **2 Timothy 2:21 (KJV)**

"The Lord shall guide thee continually… and thou shalt be like a watered garden…" – **Isaiah 58:11 (KJV)**

"For I will restore health unto thee, and I will heal thee of thy wounds, saith the Lord…" – **Jeremiah 30:17 (KJV)**

Reflection & Activation

1. What areas of my life have been broken by neglect, sin, fear, or silence?

2. What relationships need consistent rebuilding—not just apologies?

3. Where have I quit too early instead of committing to construction?

4. Have I been using words when God is asking for action?

5. Am I willing to be faithful in the process even when fruit takes time?

A Rebuilder's Prayer

Lord, I bring You the broken pieces—of my life, my leadership, my relationships, and my past. I ask You for vision to rebuild, strength to endure, and humility to learn. Let my hands do the work. Let my heart stay soft. Let my words reflect my new walk. Help me to be consistent, not just convicted. Teach me to build with wisdom, patience, and grace. Restore what was lost—not just for my benefit, but for the generations behind me. I trust You with the process. I surrender to the reconstruction. In Jesus' name, amen.

Chapter 15

When Men Stand in the Gap

Becoming the Bridge Between Brokenness and Breakthrough

"And I sought for a man among them, that should make up the hedge, and stand in the gap before me for the land..." – **Ezekiel 22:30 (KJV)**

The Place Where Most Men Go Missing

There's a sacred place in every home, church, community, and generation.

It's the place between the problem and the solution, between the pain and the promise—

It's called the gap.

God is still asking today:

"Is there a man who will stand here?"

Not a perfect man. Not a famous man

Just a willing man. A praying man. A steady man. A present man.

This chapter is a call to spiritual responsibility—to intercede, to protect, to interrupt the enemy's plans, and to cover those who are vulnerable.

What Does It Mean to Stand in the Gap?

To stand in the gap means:

You pray when others are passive

You protect when others abandon

You stay when others run

You lead when it costs you comfort

You intercede for those who can't fight for themselves

Gap men don't wait for applause—they respond to assignment.

They aren't obsessed with being seen.

They're committed to covering what God has entrusted to them.

Field Notes: The Mentor Who Interrupted a Family Curse

One man I met became the first in three generations to stay married, raise his kids, and walk in integrity.

He said:

"The men before me were good men—but they didn't know how to stand when it mattered. They ran, they shut down, or they avoided the pain. I made up my mind to be the one who would stand in the gap."

Now, his sons pray out loud.

His daughters know what covering feels like.

His wife walks in peace.

And the curse that tried to run through his bloodline stops with him.

He didn't just father his children—he fathered a new future.

Where Are Men Needed in the Gap?

1. In the Home

Stand in prayer over your wife and children.

Break the silence. Set the tone. Build a peaceful and holy atmosphere.

"As for me and my house, we will serve the Lord." – Joshua 24:15

2. In the Community

Mentor a young man. Speak up for justice. Serve your neighborhood.

You don't have to fix everything—just stand where others disappeared.

3. In the Church

Support your pastor. Lead a Bible study. Set the spiritual climate with your presence and example.

The enemy isn't scared of men who attend church. He's scared of men who pray, serve, and obey.

4. In the Culture

Stand for righteousness in a world that's falling for anything.

Let your business, behavior, and brand reflect God's Word—not just your opinion.

A gap man doesn't echo culture—he reflects the Kingdom. Characteristics of a Gap Man

Discernment: Knows when something is off and doesn't ignore it

Compassion: Covers instead of condemns

Conviction: Holds the line even when pressured to fold

Consistency: Stands even when results are slow

Covering: Prays, fasts, and fights spiritually for others

What Happens When Men Stand in the Gap?

Cycles of dysfunction are interrupted

Children grow up with direction

Wives feel safe and supported

Pastors are strengthened

Entire communities shift

Heaven responds to intercession

Hell loses ground it thought it owned

Scripture Foundation

"I have set watchmen upon thy walls, O Jerusalem, which shall never hold their peace day nor night..." – **Isaiah 62:6 (KJV)**

"The effectual fervent prayer of a righteous man availeth much." – **James 5:16 (KJV)**

"If my people... shall humble themselves, and pray... then will I hear from heaven..." – **2 Chronicles 7:14 (KJV)**

"Bear ye one another's burdens..." – **Galatians 6:2 (KJV)**

Reflection Questions

1. What gap has God been nudging me to step into—but I've avoided?

2. Have I been spiritually passive where I need to be prayerfully engaged?

3. Who in my family or community needs my intercession and presence right now?

4. What legacy would be possible if I stood firm instead of staying silent?

5. Where has God called me to interrupt dysfunction and release blessing?

A Prayer for Gap Men

Lord, make me a man who stands where others walked away. Give me strength to hold the line when others compromise. Help me intercede when others are indifferent. Teach me to cover, lead, and protect with wisdom and love. May my presence be an answer to someone's silent prayer. Let the bloodline curses stop with me. Let the blessings start through me. I will stand in the gap—with prayer, patience, and purpose. In Jesus' name, amen.

Chapter 16

When Men Speak Life

The Words That Build What Hands Cannot

"Death and life are in the power of the tongue: and they that love it shall eat the fruit thereof." – **Proverbs 18:21 (KJV)**

What You Say Is Shaping Someone's World

A man's words are not neutral—they are creative tools or destructive weapons.

You don't have to shout to be loud.

You don't have to curse to do damage.

Sometimes silence says more than anything.

This chapter is about reclaiming your voice—not just to talk—but to speak life:

Into your children

Into your spouse

Into your own mind

Into your situation

Into your legacy

Your words have power.

Your tongue is a tool.

And God wants to use it to build, heal, correct, and create.

The Silence of Fathers—and the Wounds It Left

Many men were raised without words that affirmed them.

They heard:

Criticism

Comparison

Condemnation

Or nothing at all

And that silence turned into insecurity, perfectionism, or rebellion.

Now, as grown men, many struggle to speak because:

They weren't spoken to

They fear saying the wrong thing

They equate masculinity with stoicism

They were never taught the power of a father's or husband's voice

But here's the truth:

A man who learns to speak life breaks cycles that silence created.

Field Notes: The Day the Father Started Talking

A teenage son sat in silence as his dad stared at the floor. After years of distance, absence, and discipline without dialogue, the father said:

"Son, I'm proud of you. I don't say it enough. But I see you trying, and I'm honored to be your father."

His son broke. Not because he was weak.
But because he had waited years to hear that.

That one sentence healed what 10 years of tension could not.

 The Six Realms Where Men Must Speak Life

1. Over Yourself

You can't fight the enemy while agreeing with his lies.

Speak Scripture over your mind:

"I am fearfully and wonderfully made."

"I can do all things through Christ."

"No weapon formed against me shall prosper."

2. Over Your Spouse

Don't let your wife live off of assumption.
Feed her spirit with:

"You're amazing."

"I'm grateful for you."

"You still have my heart."

"You're doing a great job."

Her confidence grows when she hears your voice.

3. Over Your Children

Speak what they need to hear—not just what you feel in
the moment.

Say:

"I believe in you."

"You are smart."

"God has a plan for your life."

"Nothing you do will make me stop loving you."

4. Over Your Circumstances

Faith doesn't deny reality—it declares truth over it.

Say:

"This isn't the end."

"God is with me."

"Better is coming."

"I still trust You, Lord."

5. Over Your Brothers

Don't just correct—encourage.

Tell another man:

"I see growth in you."

"You're not alone."

"God's hand is on your life."

6. Over the Next Generation

Don't let your legacy be silent.

Use your voice to:

Speak purpose

Set standards

Impart values

Break curses

How to Reclaim Your Voice

Start Small

You don't need a microphone. Start with one sentence:

"I love you."

"I forgive you."

"I see you."

"Let's try again."

Speak the Word

When you don't know what to say—quote Scripture.

God's Word never returns void.

Replace the Negative

Catch yourself mid-sentence:

Instead of *"I'm such a failure"* → say *"I'm still growing."*

Instead of *"They'll never change"* → say *"God can still work."*

Practice Consistency, Not Perfection

You won't always get it right—but if you show up daily with your voice, your impact will multiply.

Scripture Foundation

"Let your speech be always with grace, seasoned with salt..." – **Colossians 4:6 (KJV)**

"The Lord God hath given me the tongue of the learned, that I should know how to speak a word in season..." – **Isaiah 50:4 (KJV)**

"A wholesome tongue is a tree of life..." – **Proverbs 15:4 (KJV)**

"A word fitly spoken is like apples of gold in pictures of silver." – **Proverbs 25:11 (KJV)**

Reflection & Activation

1. Who in my life has been waiting to hear something from me?

2. What lies have I been speaking to or about myself?

3. How can I consistently encourage my family with my words?

4. Have I been too silent in areas where my voice could be a source of strength?

5. What's one way I can speak life today—before this day ends?

A Man's Prayer to Speak Life

Father, forgive me for every careless, critical, or silent moment. Teach me to speak life. Let my words reflect Your heart, not just my mood. Help me to bless my home, affirm my children, uplift my brothers, and declare truth over every situation. Break the habit of sarcasm, silence, or negativity. I surrender my tongue to You. Let it become a tool of healing, hope, and honor. In Jesus' name, amen.

Chapter 17

When Men Teach the Next Generation

Legacy Is Not What You Leave Behind—It's What You Build Into Others While You're Still Here

"We will not hide them from their children, shewing to the generation to come the praises of the Lord, and his strength, and his wonderful works that he hath done." – **Psalm 78:4 (KJV)**

They're Watching. They're Learning. What Are You Teaching?

Every man is a teacher—whether he realizes it or not.

Someone is watching how you handle anger

Someone is learning how you handle pressure

Someone is copying how you talk to women

Someone is forming their understanding of manhood based on your actions

Teaching isn't just what you say—it's what you model, what you tolerate, and what you repeat.

And here's the truth:

You don't have to be perfect to teach.

You just have to be present, honest, and intentional.

The Problem: We're Losing a Generation to Silence

We live in a time where:

Fathers are absent

Mentors are too busy

Older men are guarded

Culture is louder than character

Values are being replaced with vibes

Truth is being drowned in entertainment

And many young men and women are growing up looking for guidance in places that were never meant to shape them.

If we don't teach them—culture will.

Field Notes: The Coach Who Changed the Course

A young man, raised without a father, said his life shifted because one coach consistently showed up.

"He never gave me money. But he gave me manhood."

The coach taught him how to:

Take correction without shutting down

Speak with authority, not arrogance

Treat women with honor

Pray before decisions

Walk in humility without weakness

That young man now mentors others—not because someone gave him a manual, but because someone modeled the way.

Four Dimensions of Teaching the Next Generation

1. Teaching Through Presence

Your presence says:

"You matter. I see you. I'm here for the process."

Sit with them in discomfort

Show up to their events

Answer the phone

Remember their names

Make space for their voices

You don't need to know everything—you just need to show up.

2. Teaching Through Story

Tell your story—the real one.

Let them know your wins and your wounds

Share your mistakes without glamorizing sin

Talk about where you failed—and how God restored you

Show them what recovery looks like

Your vulnerability is someone else's survival guide.

3. Teaching Through Standards

Set the bar with love and accountability.

Teach them:

"We don't ghost people when it gets hard."

"We talk it out, not lash out."

"We walk away from fights, not from responsibility."

"We admit when we're wrong."

"We pursue purity, not popularity."

The next generation doesn't need permission to stay where they are—they need a path to grow.

4. Teaching Through Spiritual Impartation

You don't just pass down values—you pass down anointing.

Teach them how to pray

Read Scripture with them

Break generational curses by speaking blessings over them

Lay hands and declare God's Word over their future

Let them see you repent, worship, intercede, and obey

What Legacy Really Means

Legacy isn't:

A house

A business

A social media following

Legacy is:

The lives you shaped

The truths you protected

The faith you transferred

The healing you made possible

The standards you stood for

The prayers that cover them long after you're gone

Legacy means they're stronger because you stood up.

Scripture Foundation

"Train up a child in the way he should go: and when he is old, he will not depart from it." – **Proverbs 22:6 (KJV)**

"That the generation to come might know them… who should arise and declare them to their children." – **Psalm 78:6 (KJV)**

"Thou shalt teach them diligently unto thy children…" – **Deuteronomy 6:7 (KJV)**

"The things that thou hast heard of me… commit thou to faithful men, who shall be able to teach others also." – 2 **Timothy 2:2 (KJV)**

Reflection Questions

1. Who in my life is watching me right now—even if they've never said it?

2. What did I wish someone had taught me growing up—and can I teach that now?

3. Am I leaving values behind—or just valuables?

4. How can I use my past—not to impress—but to instruct?

5. What one step can I take this week to mentor, father, or guide someone younger?

A Legacy Prayer for Teaching the Next Generation

Father, thank You for trusting me with influence. I don't take it lightly. I repent for every moment I stayed silent when I should have spoken truth. I pray You'd give me clarity, courage, and consistency to teach the next generation with love, grace, and wisdom. Let my life be a sermon. Let my hands serve with humility. Let my words shape destiny. May the ones behind me rise taller because of where I stood. Let my legacy be a generation that walks in truth. In Jesus' name, amen.

Chapter 18

When Men Finish Strong

Because the End Matters More Than the Applause Along the Way

"I have fought a good fight, I have finished my course, I have kept the faith." – **2 Timothy 4:7 (KJV)**

Strength Is Proved at the End

Anyone can start strong.

But only the faithful finish well.

Too many men flame out in their:

Faith

Fatherhood

Marriage

Ministry

Assignment

Calling

The world doesn't need more men with fire at the beginning.

beginning.

It needs more men with faith at the end.

This final chapter is not about perfection.

It's about perseverance.

It's about being the kind of man who stands the test of time, doesn't fold under pressure, and crosses the finish line with honor.

Why Finishing Strong Feels So Hard

By the time you're nearing the end of a long journey—

You're often tired

You've been betrayed

You've outgrown some people

You've made mistakes

You've sacrificed in silence

You've seen doors close

You've walked through seasons of dryness and disappointment

And the temptation is to coast, quit, or compromise.

But finishing strong means:

Choosing faith when it would be easier to fold

Choosing integrity when shortcuts look faster

Choosing prayer when you don't feel spiritual

Choosing vision when your energy is low

The man who finishes well leaves behind more than memories—he leaves momentum.

Field Notes: The Elder Who Outlived the Noise

He wasn't flashy.

He didn't chase titles.

He didn't go viral.

But he:

Loved his wife for 47 years

Worked honestly

Showed up for his children

Taught young men how to lead

Finished his life with dignity and humility

At his funeral, dozens stood to testify:

"He was faithful. He didn't just show up—he stayed until the end."

That's what it means to finish strong.

How Do You Finish Strong?

1. Know What Race You're Actually Running

Don't waste time chasing approval, clout, or competition.

Focus on your God-assigned lane.

Ask: *"Am I still running the race He gave me—or one I created?"*

2. Maintain Spiritual Habits That Sustain You

Daily prayer

Time in the Word

Honest accountability

Regular reflection

Humility in correction

The men who finish strong are not the ones who had the most moments—they're the ones who had the best habits.

3. Stay Grateful, Not Entitled

You're not owed anything.

Everything you have is grace.

Don't grow bitter about what didn't happen—be thankful for what did.

Gratitude fuels endurance.

4. Serve Until the End

Don't retire from purpose.

Whether you're 35 or 75:

Someone still needs your wisdom

Someone still needs your story

Someone still needs your presence

"They shall still bring forth fruit in old age." – **Psalm 92:14 (KJV)**

5. Pass the Baton

A strong finish includes raising successors.

Teach what you've learned

Correct what you once overlooked

Impart your wisdom before the moment is gone

Finishing strong isn't about dying empty—it's about leaving others full.

What Does a Strong Finish Produce?

Peace in your soul

Honor in your name

Joy in your family

Impact in your community

Eternal reward in heaven

You don't have to finish famous.

But you must finish faithful.

Scripture Foundation

"He that shall endure unto the end, the same shall be saved." – **Matthew 24:13 (KJV)**

"Be thou faithful unto death, and I will give thee a crown of life." – **Revelation 2:10 (KJV)**

"Let us not be weary in well doing: for in due season we shall reap, if we faint not." – **Galatians 6:9 (KJV)**

"The steps of a good man are ordered by the Lord... though he fall, he shall not be utterly cast down..." – **Psalm 37:23–24 (KJV)**

Reflection & Activation

1. What unfinished area of my life is God calling me to return to?

2. Where have I been tempted to slow down or quit prematurely?

3. Who needs my voice, presence, or example to finish their own race well?

4. What small habits can I recommit to in this final stretch of the journey?

5. What legacy will my endurance make possible for those coming behind me?

A Man's Final Prayer to Finish Strong

Lord, I thank You for keeping me through every season. The ones I survived. The ones I almost quit. The ones I misunderstood. But You never left. I don't want to just start—I want to finish strong. I want to walk in faith until the final step. Lead me when I'm tired. Correct me when I'm off course. And remind me that this life is not about applause, but about obedience. Let me finish strong—with character, courage, and conviction. In Jesus' name, amen.

Final Charge: The Man Who Finishes Strong Gives the World One Last Gift—Consistency That Outlives the Crowd

You've stood through fire.

You've spoken life.

You've rebuilt.

You've led.

You've taught.

You've endured.

Now, go the distance.

Because men who stand up in every season eventually lay down in victory—knowing they gave it their all.

Finish strong.

Chapter 19

Standing When Temptation Calls

"Watch and pray, that you may not enter into temptation. The spirit indeed is willing, but the flesh is weak." – **Matthew 26:41 (ESV)**

The Battlefield Within

Every man faces a war on two fronts:

External pressures—jobs, relationships, societal expectations.

Internal struggles—lust, pride, doubt, anger.

Temptation often whispers, *"Just this once…"* and lures with promises of relief or reward. But caving in—even once—can open a door that's hard to shut.

Key Point: Victory begins by recognizing temptation not as an enemy to be ignored, but as a test to be faced head-on.

Identifying Your Personal Weak Spots

No two men fight the same battles. Some wrestle with:

1. Financial compromise (cutting corners, unethical gains)

2. Marital unfaithfulness (emotional or physical)

3. Addictive behaviors (substance, media, work)

Action Step: List your top three recurring temptations and note their triggers (time of day, people involved, emotional state).

The Three *"Watch and Pray"* Strategies

A. Vigilant Awareness

Scripture Reminder: *"Be sober, be vigilant…"* (**1 Peter 5:8**).

Keep a daily journal of your thoughts and actions. Before bed, list moments you felt tempted and what preceded them.

B. Prayerful Preparation

Scripture Reminder: *"Pray without ceasing."* (**1 Thess. 5:17**).

Begin each morning with a 5-minute *"temptation prayer"*—ask God for strength in the hours to come.

C. Practical Accountability

Scripture Foundation: *"Iron sharpens iron."* **(Prov. 27:17).**

Partner with a trusted brother. Commit to a weekly check-in on progress and struggles.

Field Note: The Man Who Refused the Shortcut

John had been offered an ***"inside deal"*** at work—easy money in exchange for ethical compromise.

He paused, prayed, and walked away.

Though he lost immediate gain, his integrity earned him a promotion six months later.

Standing firm in small moments often yields greater rewards down the road.

When You Slip: Restoration, Not Shame

Even the strongest men stumble. When you fall:

- Confess Quickly – Own your mistake before guilt festers.

- Seek Forgiveness – With God and those affected.

- Recommit to Your Guardrails – Tighten accountability and prayer.

"If we confess our sins, He is faithful and just to forgive us…" – **1 John 1:9 (NKJV)**

Building a Temptation-Proof Life

- Memorize verses that speak to your weak spots.

- Remove easy access to triggers (block websites, end harmful friendships).

- Celebrate milestones—30 days of victory warrants a small outing with your accountability partner.

Reflection & Activation

1. What temptation have I minimized in my mind?

2. Who can I enlist for consistent, prayerful accountability?

3. Which habit do I need to install or remove to protect my heart?

4. How will I restore myself if I stumble?

The Promise of Victory

"No temptation has overtaken you that is not common to man. God is faithful... He will not let you be tempted beyond your ability..." – **1 Corinthians 10:13 (ESV)**

Standing firm is not about flawless performance; it's about fighting the good fight every single day. You don't just resist temptation—you grow stronger, more resilient, more like Christ.

Finish this chapter resolved:

1.   You know your specific battlefields.

2.   You have a plan to watch, pray, and stand.

3.   You understand how to recover and grow when you fall.

Chapter 20

The Quiet Power of Consistency

Small Steps That Build an Unshakeable Legacy

"He who is faithful in a very little thing is also faithful in much." – **Luke 16:10 (NASB)**

Why Consistency Outlasts Inspiration

Enthusiasm is a spark. Consistency is the flame that endures wind, rain, and time. Any man can feel motivated for a season—to wake early, to pray fervently, to serve passionately. But true impact comes when these practices become nonnegotiable habits.

Spark vs. Steady Burn

- **Spark:** Quick flare of energy, fades without fuel.

- **Steady Burn:** Daily fuel keeps the flame alive, regardless of conditions.

When you commit to small, repeated actions—daily devotions, weekly check-ins, monthly goals—you build momentum. This momentum carries you through setbacks, fatigue, and doubt.

The Science of Habit Formation

Studies show it takes 21–66 days to solidify a new habit. But even after formation, habits need reinforcement. Understanding the habit loop helps:

Cue (Trigger)

Routine (Action)

Reward (Benefit)

Example:

- **Cue:** Your alarm rings at 5:30 AM.

- **Routine:** You read Scripture for 10 minutes.

- **Reward:** A sense of peace and clarity to start your day.

Every time you complete the loop, neural pathways strengthen, making the habit more automatic. Over time, the routine becomes part of your identity: *"I am a man who prays each morning,"* rather than *"I try to pray each morning."*

Consistency in Spiritual Disciplines

A. Daily Devotion & Prayer

1. Set a fixed time (e.g., upon waking or before bed).

2. **Use a simple plan:** 5 min. prayer, 10 min. Bible reading, 5 min. reflection.

3. **Reward yourself:** Journal one sentence of gratitude.

B. Weekly Fellowship & Accountability

1. Join a men's group or Bible study.

2. Share wins and struggles—honesty fuels growth.

3. **Assign "homework":** Pray for one another's specific needs.

C. Monthly Goal Review

4. **Track one area:** Faith, fatherhood, finances, fitness.

5. **Celebrate progress:** Even small wins deserve recognition.

6. **Course-correct:** Adjust goals if life shifts.

Field Note:

Mark, a busy pastor, started with a 5-minute daily scripture plan. Within six months, he led a small group using that same discipline—proof that consistent personal practice inevitably multiplies.

Consistency in Relationships

Trust and intimacy grow through repeated acts of love and integrity:

Spouse:

Five-minute *"check-in"* conversation

Date night or intentional outing.

Children:

Bedtime prayers.

Celebrate one achievement per week.

Colleagues & Friends:

Follow up on commitments.

A weekly prayer text or quick call.

These consistent actions say, ***"You matter,"*** more loudly than grand gestures done only once.

Consistency in Work & Calling

Whether in ministry, business, or vocation, consistency builds credibility and opportunities:

1. **Daily Excellence:** Show up on time, prepared, and fully engaged.

2. **Skill Development:** Commit to 15 minutes of learning each day (books, podcasts, courses).

3. **Network Maintenance:** Reach out to one mentor or peer weekly.

Over months and years, these habits compound. Your reputation for reliability opens doors; your growing expertise positions you as a go-to leader.

Overcoming the Thief of Consistency

A. Monotony & Boredom

Rotate formats—alternate reading plans, change fellowship venues, vary your routines.

B. Disruption & Crisis

Have *"minimums"*—if you can't do your full devotion, pray a single verse. If you can't attend group, send a text of encouragement.

Complacency & Busyness

Schedule *"consistency audits"*—monthly reminders to evaluate habits and renew commitments.

Reflection & Activation

1. Which one habit am I most inconsistent with?

2. What specific cue will trigger my new routine?

3. Who will hold me accountable each week?

4. How will I celebrate 30 days of consistency?

5. What legacy will these habits leave in my family and community?

The Legacy of Quiet Faithfulness

A man who finishes strong leaves more than accomplishments—he leaves frameworks others follow. Consistency is the blueprint:

1. Children mimic your routine and grow up valuing discipline.

2. Peers trust you as a rock in fluctuating seasons.

3. Community benefits from your steadfast service and leadership.

"Let your light so shine before men, that they may see your good works and glorify your Father in heaven." – **Matthew 5:16 (NKJV)**

Your quiet faithfulness, enacted daily, becomes a blazing testimony that points others to Christ.

Closing Charge

Don't despise the day of small beginnings. Every drop of faithful action fills the reservoir of your legacy. Embrace the quiet power of consistency—because while a firestorm of passion can burn out, a steady flame guided by discipline and grace will illuminate your path and the paths of those who follow, long after your work on earth is done.

Chapter 21

Leading Through Adversity

When the Storm Hits, The Leader Stands

"If you faint in the day of adversity, your strength is small." – **Proverbs 24:10 (KJV)**

Adversity: The Furnace of Leadership

Leadership is not tested in comfort—it's revealed in crisis.

When things fall apart—

Finances run low

Health declines

People leave

Plans collapse

—many shrink back. But a true leader leans in.

Adversity doesn't create leaders—it exposes them.

God often uses hardship as a refining fire, not to break you but to strengthen the steel of your character.

What Real Leadership Looks Like Under Pressure

When the winds blow and the ground shakes, people don't follow titles—they follow stability

True leaders:

Speak peace when others panic

Offer vision when others feel lost

Stay planted when others run

Lead prayers when others complain

Leadership is not volume—it's presence.

Being there. Standing firm. Speaking faith.

Field Notes: The Leader Who Stayed When the Lights Went Out

During a crisis that left his entire ministry underfunded and understaffed, David didn't walk away. He cut expenses, rallied volunteers, fasted weekly, and preached with fire.

Years later, his church became one of the most stable in the city. People didn't remember the lack—they remembered the man who didn't leave.

How to Lead Yourself First

Before you lead anyone else through a storm, you must lead yourself.

A. Anchor in the Word

Meditate daily on Scriptures of endurance and faith

Isaiah 43:2 – *"When you pass through the waters..."*

B. Be Honest with God

Leadership doesn't mean pretending you're okay

Pour out your emotions in prayer—frustration, fatigue, fear

C. Find a Personal Corner of Strength

A walk

A quiet room

A worship playlist

A journal

D. Find what re-centers your spirit

Leading Others When You Don't Have All the Answers

You don't need to know the outcome. You just need to be committed to the journey.

People don't need perfection from you—they need:

1. **Clarity:** *"Here's what we know."*

2. **Humility:** *"Here's what we don't."*

3. **Faith:** *"Here's what we're believing for."*

4. **Courage**: *"Here's what we're going to do."*

5. **Key Quote:** *"Crisis reveals who we trust—not what we planned."*

Guarding Your Spirit in Adversity

Adversity not only wears out your body—it wears down your spirit. That's why strong leaders:

Protect Their Inputs

Avoid gossip, doom-scrolling, or negativity

Feed on Scripture, sermons, testimonies

Limit Their Circle

Confide in the wise

Avoid the draining

Practice Rest

Even God rested after creating the world—so must you

Rest is not quitting—it's recharging to keep leading

What Leadership in Adversity Produces

1. **Respect:** People remember who showed up when it was hardest

2. **Credibility:** Words carry more weight after tested faith

3. **Growth:** Pain births purpose when submitted to God

4. **Legacy:** Leadership under fire produces faith for generations

"The fire that tried you becomes the light that guides them."

Scripture Foundation

"Blessed is the man that endureth temptation: for when he is tried, he shall receive the crown of life…" **– James 1:12 (KJV)**

"...we glory in tribulations also: knowing that tribulation worketh patience; and patience, experience; and experience, hope..." – **Romans 5:3–4 (KJV)**

"Fear thou not; for I am with thee: be not dismayed; for I am thy God..." – **Isaiah 41:10 (KJV)**

"We are troubled on every side, yet not distressed; we are perplexed, but not in despair; Persecuted, but not forsaken; cast down, but not destroyed." – **2 Corinthians 4:8–9 (KJV)**

Reflection & Activation

1. What adversity am I currently facing that's testing my leadership?

2. Am I reacting in fear, frustration, or faith?

3. Who is looking to me for calm and clarity in this season?

4. What Scriptures anchor me when storms come?

5. How will I protect my emotional and spiritual reserves during this time

A Leader's Prayer in the Storm

Lord,

You see every wave, every pressure, every weight I carry.

Remind me that You are still in control—even when I don't understand.

Give me the strength to lead with peace, the wisdom to lead with truth,

and the humility to say, *"I need You."*

Let me be a shelter for others—not because I'm perfect,

but because I'm planted in You.

I don't ask for easy days—only for Your presence in the hardest ones.

In Jesus' name,

Amen.

Final Charge: Lead Through the Fire, Not Around It

You don't have to be the loudest in the room.

You don't have to have all the answers.

But you do have to be present.

Steady.

Faithful.

When others fall back, step forward.

When others hide, speak truth.

When others complain, pray louder.

Because men who lead through adversity don't just survive the storm—they build lighthouses for others to find the shore.

Finish strong.

Chapter 22

The Gift of Servant Leadership

Leading with Humility, Loving with Strength

"But he that is greatest among you shall be your servant." – **Matthew 23:11 (KJV)**

Redefining Greatness

In the world's eyes, leadership often means being in charge, standing at the top, and calling the shots. But Jesus flipped the definition. In His kingdom, the greatest leader is not the loudest voice or the most visible name—it's the one who stoops to serve.

Servant leadership is not weakness. It's strength wrapped in humility. It's authority exercised through care. It's power submitted to purpose.

"For even the Son of man came not to be ministered unto, but to minister..." – **Mark 10:45 (KJV)**

Why Servant Leadership Is Rare and Powerful

Servant leadership takes work. It means:

Listening more than speaking

Valuing people over platforms

Choosing sacrifice over spotlight

It's easier to command than to care. It's simpler to instruct than to invest. But true leaders don't just give orders—they give themselves.

Servant leaders leave a legacy because they lift others up—not build empires for themselves.

The Model of Christ

Jesus washed feet.

He fed crowds.

He healed outcasts.

He carried the cross.

And He did it all not because He had to—but because He loved.

If anyone had the right to demand service, it was Christ. But He chose to kneel.

"Let this mind be in you, which was also in Christ Jesus... and took upon him the form of a servant." – **Philippians 2:5–7 (KJV)**

That's your model. That's our calling.

Field Notes: The Boss Who Served the Janitor

A business owner once noticed his janitor working late and exhausted. Quietly, he grabbed a mop and helped him finish cleaning the floor. The next day, word spread among the staff—not because he boasted, but because his action echoed louder than any policy memo.

Over time, turnover decreased, and company morale skyrocketed. Why? Because servant leadership creates culture. It sets the tone.

What Servant Leaders Do Differently

A. They See the Invisible

- They notice the one who didn't speak up.

- They check in on the person everyone overlooks.

- They value the people who can't offer anything in return.

B. They Do the Small Things

They refill the coffee.

They wipe the table.

They carry the bag.

C. They Ask Better Questions

"How can I support you?"

"What do you need from me?"

"How can I make this easier for you?"

6. Servant Leadership in Every Role

At Home:

Help with the dishes.

Pray with your spouse.

Do the task nobody wants.

At Work:

Be early.

Stay late when needed.

Celebrate others' wins more than your own.

In Ministry:

Don't just teach—listen.

Don't just lead—lift.

Don't just correct—care.

What It Costs—and What It Gives

Yes, servant leadership costs something.

Your pride

Your convenience

Your comfort

But it gives something greater:

1. **Trust:** People follow those who serve them.

2. **Respect:** You don't have to demand it—you'll earn it.

3. **Multiplication:** When you serve others, they serve others too.

"And whosoever of you will be the chiefest, shall be servant of all." – **Mark 10:44 (KJV)**

Scripture Foundation

"He that is greatest among you shall be your servant." – **Matthew 23:11 (KJV)**

"By love serve one another." – **Galatians 5:13 (KJV)**

"Be kindly affectioned one to another... in honour preferring one another." – **Romans 12:10 (KJV)**

"And whosoever shall compel thee to go a mile, go with him twain." – **Matthew 5:41 (KJV)**

Reflection & Activation

1. Where am I still leading for recognition instead of service?

2. Who in my life needs my time, not just my instruction?

3. What small acts of service have I been ignoring or delegating?

4. How can I build a culture of servant leadership in my home or team?

5. When people speak of my leadership, what will they remember—my power or my presence?

A Servant Leader's Prayer

Lord,

Thank You for showing me what true leadership looks like—not from a throne, but from a towel.

Help me to lead like You—with humility, with kindness, with courage.

Let me never get so important that I forget to serve.

Let my leadership be love in motion.

When the world pushes for position, let me choose people.

When the spotlight calls, let me choose the cross.

Make me a leader worth following—not because of my strength, but because of my surrender.

In Jesus' name,

Amen.

Final Charge: To Serve Is to Lead

You don't need a mic to lead.

You don't need a title to influence.

You just need a heart willing to stoop low enough to lift someone else.

Because in the kingdom of God, the men who stoop low are the ones God lifts high.

And the men who serve today shape the world tomorrow.

Finish strong—by starting with service.

Chapter 23

Cultivating Spiritual Resilience

Staying Rooted When Life Tries to Shake You

"Blessed is the man that trusteth in the Lord… he shall be as a tree planted by the waters… and shall not be careful in the year of drought." – **Jeremiah 17:7–8 (KJV)**

What Is Spiritual Resilience?

Spiritual resilience is not the absence of struggle. It's the strength to keep trusting, standing, and believing—even when everything around you is falling apart.

It's that inner grit that refuses to quit.

It's that quiet endurance that holds the line.

It's that unwavering faith that says, "God is still with me."

Resilient men don't avoid storms. They survive them. They stand tall through them. And they grow stronger because of them.

Why Spiritual Resilience Matters

Life will test you.

Disappointments will come.

Doors will close.

Prayers won't be answered immediately.

People will betray or abandon you.

And if your faith is shallow, you'll fold. But when you're deeply rooted in God, storms don't destroy you—they develop you.

"When thou passest through the waters, I will be with thee…" – **Isaiah 43:2 (KJV)**

You can't choose your storms, but you can choose your foundation.

What Makes a Man Spiritually Strong?

A. Consistent Devotion

Time in the Word

Daily prayer

Worship, even in pain

B. Holy Spirit Dependence

Listening to His promptings

Yielding, not striving

Trusting more than calculating

C. Community & Accountability

Walking with other resilient men

Receiving correction

Being encouraged when weary

D. Long-Term Perspective

Resilient men don't live for applause—they live for eternity.

They ask, "Will this matter in 50 years? Will it matter in heaven?"

Field Notes: The Man Who Kept Showing Up

Tim lost his job, faced a health scare, and buried his father—all in the same year. But every Sunday, he showed up to church. Every morning, he opened his Bible. He didn't shout. He didn't post about it. He just stayed faithful.

Five years later, he became a spiritual mentor to young men going through their own storms. Why? Because he didn't just survive—he stood.

Five Practices That Build Resilience

1. Anchor in the Word

"Thy word have I hid in mine heart, that I might not sin against thee." – **Psalm 119:11 (KJV)**

Read a chapter a day.

Memorize one verse per week.

2. Pray Honestly, Not Perfectly

God can handle your raw.

David's psalms were often messy but real.

3. Fast Occasionally

Fasting re-centers your heart.

It weakens the flesh and strengthens the spirit.

Speak Life, Not Death

"Death and life are in the power of the tongue…" – **Proverbs 18:21 (KJV)**

Declare Scripture over your life—even when you don't feel it.

Keep a Journal of God's Faithfulness

- Write down past answered prayers.

- Revisit them when doubt creeps in.

What Resilience Produces in You

- **Maturity:** You're no longer moved by every emotion.

- **Wisdom:** You see the big picture, not just the pain.

- **Authority:** Your voice carries weight because it's been through fire.

- **Peace:** Not because things are easy—but because you know God is with you.

"They that wait upon the Lord shall renew their strength..." – **Isaiah 40:31 (KJV)**

What to Do When You Feel Spiritually Dry

- **Don't disconnect:** Dryness is not a sign to quit—it's a sign to press in.

- **Revisit your spiritual roots**: What first ignited your faith?

- **Speak to your soul:** Like David, say, *"Why art thou cast down, O my soul? Hope thou in God."* **– Psalm 42:5 (KJV)**

- **Stay planted:** A dry season doesn't mean God has left. Stay in community, stay in prayer, stay faithful.

Scripture Foundation

"We are troubled on every side, yet not distressed; we are perplexed, but not in despair." **– 2 Corinthians 4:8 (KJV)**

"He shall be like a tree planted by the rivers of water…" **– Psalm 1:3 (KJV)**

"My brethren, count it all joy when ye fall into divers temptations; knowing this, that the trying of your faith worketh patience." **– James 1:2–3 (KJV)**

"Endure hardness, as a good soldier of Jesus Christ." **– 2 Timothy 2:3 (KJV)**

Reflection & Activation

1. What current trial is testing my spiritual roots?

2.   Have I been reactive or rooted during hardship?

3.   What daily spiritual practice do I need to return to?

4.   Who can I walk with to stay spiritually anchored?

5.   What promise from God will I hold onto this week?

A Prayer for Endurance

Lord,

Help me to stand when everything around me shakes.

Make me rooted, not reactive.

Planted, not panicked.

Let my faith run deeper than my feelings.

Grow in me the kind of strength that can't be stolen.

The kind of peace that isn't dependent on comfort.

Teach me to endure, to hope, to wait, and to trust—

even in the valley.

Let my life be like a tree—

bearing fruit even in drought,

and pointing upward even in darkness.

In Jesus' name,

Amen.

Final Charge: Resilience Is Your Legacy

You don't have to be flashy to be faithful.

You don't need a perfect record to be resilient.

You just have to stay rooted.

Show up. Stand firm. Trust God.

Let the storms come.

Let the winds howl.

Because the men who build deep roots outlast every season—and feed generations to come.

Finish strong—by standing strong.

Chapter 24

Building Brotherhood

Because No Man Finishes Strong Alone

"Iron sharpeneth iron; so a man sharpeneth the countenance of his friend." – **Proverbs 27:17 (KJV)**

The Lie of Lone Manhood

Culture tells men to be strong, silent, and self-sufficient.

"Don't ask for help."

"Don't show weakness."

"Don't depend on anyone."

But Scripture tells a different story.

From Genesis to Revelation, we see men walking together—Moses and Joshua, David and Jonathan, Paul and Timothy, Jesus and His disciples.

Biblical manhood was never meant to be isolated—it was always meant to be relational.

Why Brotherhood Matters

A. Encouragement in Trials

When life hits hard, a brother reminds you:

You're not alone.

This isn't the end.

God is still working.

B. Accountability in Weakness

A real brother doesn't just hype you up—he holds you up.

He asks tough questions.

He challenges your excuses.

He prays you through temptations.

C. Celebration in Progress

When you win, he claps the loudest.

Not out of competition, but out of covenant.

"Two are better than one… for if they fall, the one will lift up his fellow." – **Ecclesiastes 4:9–10 (KJV)**

Field Notes: The Friendship That Saved a Life

When James battled depression, he almost gave up on everything—his faith, his marriage, his life. But one brother noticed he hadn't shown up to their weekly prayer call. He drove across town, sat in silence with James, and cried with him.

That moment didn't fix everything. But it kept James alive long enough for God to bring healing.

Brotherhood doesn't always have answers—but it never leaves you alone.

What Makes a Brotherhood Strong

1. Shared Faith

Centered on Christ, not hobbies or convenience.

Built on truth, not flattery.

2. Mutual Trust

What's shared stays sacred.

Vulnerability is honored, not weaponized.

3. Consistent Presence

Real brothers don't disappear when things get uncomfortable.

They check in, show up, and stay.

4. Spiritual Pursuit

They pray together.

Study the Word together.

Fast together when one is in crisis.

How to Find (and Keep) Brotherhood

A. Be the Friend You're Looking For

Text first.

Pray for them without being asked.

Celebrate their success like it's your own.

B. Initiate Community

Don't wait for perfect conditions—start where you are.

Invite two brothers to meet monthly for breakfast and prayer.

Share your story first—honesty breeds connection.

C. Deal With Offense Quickly

Brotherhood breaks when egos are bigger than grace.

Forgive quickly.

Talk directly, not through others.

Value the bond more than the moment.

"A friend loveth at all times, and a brother is born for adversity." – **Proverbs 17:17 (KJV)**

Brotherhood in Marriage and Fatherhood

A man connected to strong brotherhood becomes:

1. A better husband (because he has men to sharpen him)

2. A better father (because he's not parenting from an empty tank)

3. A better leader (because he has covering and counsel)

Isolated men make impulsive decisions.

Connected men make wiser ones.

Building Brotherhood Across Generations

Elders need young men to pass wisdom to.

Younger men need elders to guide them.

Brotherhood is not just horizontal—it's generational.

Start a culture of connection with the men behind and ahead of you.

"The things that thou hast heard of me... commit thou to faithful men..." – **2 Timothy 2:2 (KJV)**

Scripture Foundation

"Bear ye one another's burdens, and so fulfil the law of Christ." – **Galatians 6:2 (KJV)**

"Confess your faults one to another, and pray one for another..." – **James 5:16 (KJV)**

"Behold, how good and how pleasant it is for brethren to dwell together in unity!" – **Psalm 133:1 (KJV)**

Reflection & Activation

1. Who are my current spiritual brothers? Am I truly connected or just casually acquainted?

2. Who is a brother I need to reach out to today?

3. What area of my life have I been hiding out of fear of judgment?

4. What could change in my spiritual walk if I surrounded myself with godly men?

5. What steps can I take to start or join a consistent men's group this month?

A Brother's Prayer

Lord,

Thank You for not calling me to walk alone.

Forgive me for believing I had to carry everything by myself.

Help me to be the kind of brother who lifts, not competes…

Who stays, not disappears…

Who listens, not lectures.

Teach me to open up without fear…

To love without condition…

And to sharpen without pride.

Build in me the kind of brotherhood that leaves no man behind.

In Jesus' name,

Amen.

Final Charge: Brotherhood Isn't Optional—It's Oxygen

Isolation will starve your spirit.

Ego will block your breakthrough.

But brotherhood?

It will carry you when your strength runs out.

Don't wait until the fire comes to find your tribe.

Build it now. Strengthen it today.

Because when the storm hits, the man with brothers never fights alone.

Finish strong—together.

Chapter 25

Empowering Tomorrow's Leaders

Investing in the Next Generation to Finish Strong

"And the things that thou hast heard of me among many witnesses, the same commit thou to faithful men, who shall be able to teach others also." – **2 Timothy 2:2 (KJV)**

The Urgent Call to Develop Leaders

The world of ministry, business, family, and community needs leaders—men of integrity, vision, and faith. Yet too often, we focus on our own performance and neglect the vital task of raising the next generation. Empowering tomorrow's leaders isn't an optional extra; it's a sacred responsibility. When a man finishes strong, his ultimate legacy is not the ministry he built or the fortune he amassed, but the men he equipped to carry the torch forward.

Leadership development is not accidental. It requires intentional strategy, time investment, and spiritual nudging. Just as a farmer tills soil, plants seed, and nurtures growth, so must we cultivate potential in younger men through teaching, modeling, and entrusting responsibility.

The Biblical Mandate for Discipleship

Scripture overflows with examples of leaders mentoring others:

1. **Moses to Joshua:** After leading Israel, Moses spent decades preparing Joshua—teaching him God's laws, modeling faith under fire, and entrusting him with authority (Deut. 31:7–8).

2. **Elijah to Elisha:** Elijah's life and ministry became a classroom for Elisha, who received a "double portion" of his spirit (2 Kings 2).

3. **Paul to Timothy and Titus:** Paul invested in Timothy from a young age—teaching doctrine, encouraging perseverance, and commissioning him to lead churches (1 Tim. 1:2; 2 Tim. 2:2).

"Discipleship is multiplication—teaching faithful men who teach others."

Why Empowerment, Not Just Instruction

Instruction imparts knowledge; empowerment entrusts authority. A leader who only teaches leaves disciples dependent. A leader who empowers releases them into responsibility and growth:

- **Instruction-Alone Pitfall**: Men learn principles but lack real-world application.

- **Empowerment Advantage:** Men learn by doing—under guidance, with accountability, and in community.

Empowerment nurtures confidence, ownership, and innovation. When you hand a younger man a task, you signal trust in his giftings and character. You communicate: *"I believe you can finish strong too."*

Field Notes: From Student to Shepherd

Case Study: When Pastor Andrew launched a small Bible study, he invited two young men, Joel and Marcus, to co-lead weekly sessions. At first, they stumbled—missed cues, weak transitions, nervous delivery. Andrew provided immediate feedback, prayer support, and modeling. Within six months, Joel preached his first sermon; Marcus organized outreach events.

Outcome: Both now serve full-time—Joel as a youth pastor, Marcus as a campus ministry leader. They credit Andrew's early empowerment as the foundation of their calling.

The Four Phases of Leadership Development

A. Identify Potential

1. **Observe Character:** Faithfulness in small things, integrity under pressure, humility in success.

2. **Spot Gifts:** Teaching ease, hospitality, creative problem-solving, administrative aptitude.

3. **Engage Interest:** Invite input, ask for help, gauge passion.

B. Instruct and Equip

1. **Teach Core Principles:** God's Word, leadership values, ministry methods.

2. **Provide Resources:** Books, training workshops, online courses, mentorship relationships.

3. **Model Excellence:** Demonstrate punctuality, preparation, prayer, and compassion.

C. Entrust Responsibility

1. **Assign Tasks:** Lead a meeting, teach a lesson, manage an event, handle finances.

2. **Set Expectations:** Clarity on objectives, deadlines, and quality standards.

3. **Offer Authority:** Let them make decisions, with agreed guardrails.

D. Evaluate and Release

1. **Debrief and Feedback:** Celebrate successes, address gaps, adjust strategies.

2. **Increase Scope:** Gradually expand their sphere of influence and responsibility.

3. **Release to Leadership:** Commission publicly, endorse their authority, step back.

4. **Promise:** *"As we invest in others, we build a kingdom that outlasts our own tenure."*

Practical Strategies for Empowering Leaders

Regular One-on-One Meetings

Weekly check-ins to pray together, review progress, and address obstacles.

Leadership Training Cohort

Small groups that study leadership principles, practice public speaking, and role-play conflict resolution.

Shadowing Opportunities

Let emerging leaders accompany you to meetings, negotiations, pastoral visits, or decision-making sessions.

Project-Based Leadership

Assign a specific initiative—community service project, worship event, small group launch—complete with budget, timeline, and reporting.

Peer Accountability Groups

Form triads of emerging leaders who pray for each other, hold one another accountable, and share insights weekly.

Celebrate Milestones Publicly

Commission new leaders with prayer, certificates, or a public blessing to reinforce their authority and encourage the congregation.

Overcoming Common Challenges

1. Fear of Delegation:

Start small. Delegate low-risk tasks and build trust through consistent follow-up.

2. Impatience with Progress:

Remember that character development takes time. Celebrate incremental wins.

3. Protecting Ego:

Keep the focus on God's work, not personal recognition. View leadership multiplication as your greatest achievement.

4. Conflict Among Leaders:

Address friction immediately. Model reconciliation, clarify roles, and reinforce shared mission.

What Empowerment Produces

1. **Sustainable Growth:** Ministries and businesses thrive when leadership pipelines are robust.

2. **Innovation:** Fresh leaders bring new ideas, creativity, and energy.

3. **Resilience:** Shared responsibility prevents burnout in any one leader.

4. **Legacy:** Your influence multiplies as empowered leaders invest in others.

"Many hands make light work; many leaders make lasting impact."

Scripture Foundation

"And he gave some, apostles; and some, prophets; and some, evangelists; and some, pastors and teachers; for the perfecting of the saints..." – **Ephesians 4:11–12 (KJV)**

"Feed my lambs... feed my sheep." – **John 21:15–16 (KJV)**

"He that is greatest among you shall be your servant." – **Matthew 23:11 (KJV)**

"Let the elders who rule well be counted worthy of double honor..." – **1 Timothy 5:17 (KJV)**

Reflection & Activation

1. Who are the top three men you see potential in?

2. What specific giftings has God placed in them?

3. Which phase of development are they currently in—identify, equip, entrust, or release?

4. What is one concrete step you will take this week to advance their leadership?

5. How will you publicly recognize their growing authority to reinforce their confidence?

A Prayer for Emerging Leaders

Lord,

Thank You for calling men into Your service.

Give me eyes to see potential, wisdom to equip them, and courage to entrust them with responsibility.

Help me to lead with humility—knowing that Your work through them is greater than what I do alone.

Build character in their hearts, competence in their skills, and compassion in their souls.

Let them finish strong, and then carry forward the legacy You've entrusted to me.

In Jesus' name,

Amen.

Final Charge: Empowerment Is the Treasure You Leave Behind

Your greatest inheritance isn't wealth or fame.

It's men and women who bear godly fruit because you invested in them.

Don't hoard responsibility.

Don't fear being outshined.

Release the next generation with prayer, vision, and authority.

Because the man who finishes strong isn't the one who stands alone—

He's the one whose influence echoes in the lives of those he empowered.

Finish strong—by empowering others to finish stronger.

Chapter 26

Living Beyond the Finish Line

A Legacy That Outlasts Your Lifetime

"I have fought a good fight, I have finished my course, I have kept the faith." – **2 Timothy 4:7 (KJV)**

The Finish Line Isn't the End

For many, *"finish strong"* conjures an image of crossing a ribbon, celebrating victory, and drawing a line under a race. But God's calling doesn't end at the finish line—it extends beyond it. Living beyond the finish line means your influence, your values, and your faith continue to impact others long after you've stepped off the stage. It's about building an enduring legacy that glorifies God, blesses your family, and equips future generations for their own races.

The finish line marked by applause is temporary. A legacy marked by transformed lives is eternal. As men called to finish strong, our greatest task is not merely to close our own chapter but to open new chapters for those who follow.

The Difference Between a Race and a Relay

- **A race is solitary:** one man against time and terrain. **A relay is communal:** one generation passing the baton to the next. Christianity reframes life as a relay, not a solo sprint.

- **Self-focused race:** *"How well did I do?"*

- **God-focused relay:** *"Who will carry this forward?"*

Our goal is not to finish first but to finish well—and then hand off God's truth, love, and purpose to faithful men who will run on.

"The things that thou hast heard of me… commit thou to faithful men, who shall be able to teach others also." – **2 Timothy 2:2 (KJV)**

Field Notes: The Man Who Became a Platform

Pastor James led a vibrant church of 2,000. When he retired, the congregation feared decline. But because he spent decades equipping leaders—elders, deacons, teaching teams—the church not only survived but thrived under new pastors. His finish line was not his last sermon but the leaders he left behind.

Your calling extends through the lives you touch and develop.

Four Pillars of Lasting Legacy

To live beyond your finish line, invest deliberately in four areas:

A. Family Foundations

1. **Spiritual Heritage:** Pass down faith through daily devotions, bedtime prayers, and family worship.

2. **Character Inheritance:** Demonstrate honesty, generosity, and humility—values children absorb by watching, not by hearing lectures.

3. **Storytelling:** Share family history and God's faithfulness across generations, anchoring identity in God's work

B. Leadership Multiplication

1. **Mentorship Networks:** Create structures where older men mentor middle-aged men who mentor younger men.

2. **Training Resources:** Leave behind books, sermon recordings, training manuals, and strategic plans.

3. **Public Commissioning:** Formally endorse new leaders, giving them authority and confidence to step into roles.

C. Institutional Structures

1. **Church or Ministry Systems:** Establish ministries, small groups, budgets, and governance that outlast any one leader.

2. **Business Succession Plans:** In family businesses or nonprofit ventures, develop clear leadership pipelines and financial stewardship guidelines.

3. **Scholarship or Endowment Funds:** Finance future ministries or educational opportunities that perpetuate your vision.

D. Cultural Impact

1. **Public Witness:** Use your platform—blogs, social media, speaking engagements—to articulate values that influence culture.

2. **Philanthropy:** Support causes and organizations that align with your convictions, ensuring your influence endures through strategic giving.

3. **Creative Works:** Write books, record music, create art that continues to speak truth long after you're gone.

Overcoming Obstacles to a Lasting Legacy

1. Short-Term Focus

- **Pitfall:** Chasing immediate results at the expense of future impact.

- **Solution:** Balance urgent tasks with strategic investments—daily discipleship, long-term teaching, and mentoring schedules.

2. Ego and Control

- **Pitfall:** Reluctance to release authority or admit successors may outshine you.

- **Solution:** Embrace humility—celebrate others' gifts, delegate fully, and guard against pride.

3. Lack of Succession Planning

- **Pitfall:** No clear roadmap for who leads next.

- **Solution:** Identify and develop leaders early; write transition documents and hold commissioning ceremonies.

4. Failure to Document

- **Pitfall:** Years of wisdom remain in memories, not in manuals.

- **Solution:** Record sermons, write journals, video leadership lessons, and create digital archives.

6. Practical Steps to Launch Your Legacy Plan

Conduct a Legacy Audit

1. List every area where you lead—home, church, workplace.

2. Identify who is ready to step up and who needs more equipping.

Create a Development Calendar

1. Schedule monthly leadership workshops.

2. Plan quarterly family retreats centered on faith and character.

Draft a Succession Blueprint

1. Define roles, responsibilities, and timelines for handing off key tasks.

2. Communicate the plan with transparency to all stakeholders.

Document Your Journey

1. Begin writing your spiritual autobiography—key lessons, turning points, answered prayers.

2. Encourage protégés to record their learning and testimonies.

Commission the Next Generation

1. Host a public service or meeting where you formally commission emerging leaders.

2. Pray over them, lay on hands, issue mission statements for their season of ministry.

Establish Enduring Resources

1. Set up a scholarship fund in your name to support future ministry leaders.

2. Create a digital library of teachings, accessible to anyone, anywhere.

What Living Beyond the Finish Line Looks Like

- **Generational Faith Continuity:** Children and grandchildren know your God-story and carry it forward.

- **Sustained Ministry Impact:** The church or organization you founded continues to grow and bless communitie

- **Cultivated Leaders:** A cohort of men and women serve in diverse roles, equipped by your investment.

- **Cultural Influence:** Your writings or recordings still resonate and shape public discourse.

Scripture Foundation

"They that be wise shall shine as the brightness of the firmament; and they that turn many to righteousness as the stars forever and ever." – **Daniel 12:3 (KJV)**

"For I have no man likeminded who will naturally care for your state." – **Philippians 2:20 (KJV)**

"And Jesus increased in wisdom and stature, and in favour with God and man." – **Luke 2:52 (KJV)**

"Then shall the righteous shine forth as the sun in the kingdom of their Father." – **Matthew 13:43 (KJV)**

Legacy Principle: *"Turn many to righteousness—shining stars in God's galaxy."*

Reflection & Activation

1. What elements of my life will outlive me?

2. Who have I already started equipping—and who still needs my investment?

3. What resources (time, money, expertise) can I set aside for future leaders?

4. When will I host our first commissioning service?

5. How can I ensure my family carries our spiritual heritage for generations?

A Prayer for Enduring Influence

Eternal God,

Thank You for every step of this journey.

Help me to see beyond my finish line—into the generations You're calling.

Give me wisdom to equip others well, courage to release them fully, and grace to celebrate their growth.

Let my life's work not fade away but multiply into a harvest of faithful men and women.

May the seeds I sow today bear fruit a hundredfold in Your kingdom.

In Jesus' name,

Amen.

Final Charge: Your Legacy Is Your Final Sermon

You will preach your last sermon—through the lives you've shaped.

Your final message won't be on a pulpit but in the hearts of those you invested in.

'Don't wait until you retire.

Start today—but structure it for tomorrow.

Empower tomorrow's leaders.

Equip them.

Entrust them.

So that when you cross your final finish line, the race continues—

faster, stronger, and deeper—carrying the torch you once held.

Finish strong—and begin the next chapter in others.

Chapter 27

Passing the Torch with Purpose

Ensuring the Flame of Faith Burns Bright for Generations

"And the things that thou hast heard of me among many witnesses, the same commit thou to faithful men, who shall be able to teach others also." – **2 Timothy 2:2 (KJV)**

The Sacred Duty of Succession

After decades of running your race, facing trials, and standing firm, you arrive at a pivotal moment: the completion of your season of primary leadership. Yet the story does not end with your final act. Rather, you pass the torch—entrusting your vision, values, and spiritual momentum into capable hands. This act of succession is more than logistics; it is a spiritual mandate. Without purposeful handoff, legacies fade, ministries stall, and families weaken. With intentional succession, the torch of faith burns brighter, carried forward by those you have equipped.

"Your greatest achievement is not your own victory—but the victories nurtured in those you lead."

The Biblical Blueprint for Passing the Torch

A. Moses to Joshua

Moses spent 40 years leading Egypt, 40 years in exile, then 40 years guiding Israel. In his final days, he poured wisdom into Joshua—teaching him law (Deut. 31), modeling intercession, and publicly commissioning him (Deut. 34).

B. Elijah to Elisha

Before Elijah was taken, Elisha asked for—and received—a double portion of Elijah's spirit (2 Kings 2). Elijah's mantle fell, symbolizing authority transfer and divine empowerment.

C. Paul to Timothy & Titus

Paul invested in Timothy from youth— entrusting him with letters, encouraging him in hardship, and defining his role **(1 Tim. 1:2; 2 Tim. 2:2).**

Pattern: Identify—Equip—Empower—Commission—Release.

Why Passing the Torch Requires Intention

- **Avoiding Leadership Vacuum:** Without a plan, organizations stall; families lack vision.

- **Preventing Burnout:** Successors share the load, ensuring sustainability.

- **Honoring Your Season—and God's Timing:** Recognize when to lead and when to let go.

- **Fulfilling God's Design for Multiplication:** Jesus sent disciples to make disciples **(Matt. 28:19–20).**

"Multiplication is God's method for immortality."

Field Notes: A Smooth Handoff vs. a Sudden Departure

Smooth Handoff: Pastor Samuel began mentoring his assistant five years before retirement. They co-led services, the assistant crafted sermons under Samuel's feedback, and gradually assumed leadership in small groups. When Samuel stepped down, the congregation already embraced the new pastor.

Sudden Departure: When Director Michael left due to health issues without preparation, the nonprofit floundered—programs canceled, staff morale plummeted, and donors withdrew until an interim leader emerged months later.

Lesson: Intentional transition prevents chaos.

The Five Phases of Purposeful Succession

Vision Casting

- **Clarify Your Core Values & Mission:** Write a clear, concise statement that defines why you began and where you're headed.

- **Communicate Transparently:** Share your retirement or transition timeline with stakeholders—family, staff, congregation, board.

Talent Identification

- **Observe Character & Competence:** Who demonstrates integrity, skill, and calling?

- **Solicit Recommendations:** Invite input from trusted peers—elders, board members, coworkers.

Development & Shadowing

- **Assign Growing Responsibilities:** Let potential successors lead projects, handle crises, and represent you in meetings.

- **Provide Resources:** Training, conferences, coaching, spiritual retreats.

Encourage Questions & Feedback: Cultivate humility and teachable spirit.

Public Commissioning

- **Ceremony of Authority Transfer:** A special service or meeting where you lay hands, speak blessing, and officially declare their role.

- **Document the Transition:** Create written agreements, job descriptions, and vision covenants.

Stepping Back & Supporting

- **Allow Autonomy:** Resist the urge to micromanage; offer counsel—but let them lead.

- **Maintain Mentorship Role:** Remain available as advisor and prayer partner.

- **Celebrate New Leadership:** Cheer successes publicly, reinforcing trust in the new leader.

Practical Tools for a Successful Transition

Succession Timeline Template

Map out milestones over 12–24 months—training, co-leading, commissioning, handoff date.

Leadership Competency Checklist

Evaluate on integrity, vision casting, decision-making, pastoral care, administrative skill.

Transition Communication Plan

Schedule announcements, Q&A sessions, informational packets for stakeholder

Mentor-Mentee Agreement

Outline expectations, meeting frequency, confidentiality terms, success metrics.

Legacy Documentation

Spiritual autobiography, doctrinal statements, ministry philosophies, key contacts, financial processes.

Addressing Common Succession Challenges

A. Fear of Obsolescence

Your legacy is secured through those you empower, not your continued presence.

B. Pride & Control

Focus on God's mission—if the work thrives, it honors Him and you.

C. Successor Resistance

Engage early; clarify vision; listen to their insights and concerns; foster ownership.

D. Stakeholder Doubt

Publicly affirm the successor's calling; share success stories from the development phase.

The Spiritual Dimension of Passing the Torch

Passing leadership isn't merely administrative—it's deeply spiritual:

1. **Prayer of Impartation:** Invoke God's anointing on the successor.

2. **Spiritual Warfare:** Recognize that transitions draw spiritual opposition; mobilize prayer networks.

3. **Legacy Prayers:** Pray for continued faithfulness, perseverance, and divine wisdom for the next generation.

"The transfer of authority is sealed in prayer."

What a Purposeful Transition Produces

1. **Continuity of Mission:** The organization or family retains focus and momentum.

2. **Healthier Relationships:** Clear roles prevent conflict and confusion.

3. **Renewed Vision:** Fresh leadership often brings new ideas and revitalized energy.

4. **Strengthened Legacy:** Your influence extends well beyond your active years.

"A well-passed baton multiplies the race's impact."

Scripture Foundation

"The things which thou hast heard... commit thou to faithful men, who shall be able to teach others also." – **2 Timothy 2:2 (KJV)**

"Where there is no vision, the people perish..." – **Proverbs 29:18 (KJV)**

"Without counsel purposes are disappointed: but in the multitude of counsellors they are established." – **Proverbs 15:22 (KJV)**

"I have planted, Apollos watered; but God gave the increase." – **1 Corinthians 3:6 (KJV)**

Reflection & Activation

1. What is my personal transition timeline?

2. Who are my top two successors, and have I started their development?

3. What documents and resources must I create or update for their success?

4. When will I host the commissioning ceremony?

5. How will I continue to pray and support after my active leadership ends?

A Prayer for Passing the Torch

Almighty God,

Thank You for every season of leadership You entrusted to me.

Now I surrender the baton to those You have prepared.

Fill them with vision, courage, and wisdom.

Let my years of triumph and trials serve as a guide, not a crutch.

May Your Spirit flow through them, accomplishing more than I could imagine.

Bind us together in purpose and love.

Protect us from pride, fear, and division.

And may this handoff advance Your kingdom, ushering in an era of greater fruitfulness.

In Jesus' name,

Amen.

Final Charge: Your Greatest Legacy Is the Leaders You Release

Your life's work finds its true meaning in the generations you empower.

Don't cling to the stage—shine on those who follow.

Release them with prayer, trust, and clear vision.]

Because the man who finishes strong is not the one who stands alone—but the one whose influence multiplies, who sows faithful seeds, and watches new fields flourish.

Finish strong—and pass the torch with purpose.

Rise and Stand

A Call to Courage

Brothers,

Today you are invited to rise—to stand firm in the face of doubt, to speak truth when silence is easier, and to lead with courage when the world around you trembles. Standing up isn't just a single moment of boldness; it's a daily decision to honor your values, protect those you love, and shape the world for good.

When you stand up—against injustice, against fear, against the whisper of compromise—you show what real strength looks like. You remind yourself that your voice matters, your actions matter, and your faith empowers you to move mountains. Embrace the call to courage, lean into vulnerability, and trust that every small stand paves the way for greater breakthroughs.

May this chapter encourage you to stand tall in your convictions, extend your hand to those who need your support, and shine as a beacon of integrity. When men stand up, they inspire others to rise alongside them—and together, we build something unshakable.

Stand strong. Stand true. Stand up.

— Lemuel King